Candy Basics

Introduction

Candy making is a lot of fun as a family or group project. There are methods and tips that can help you achieve consistent, successful results. Here are a few basic ideas.

Temperature

A good candy thermometer is very important to successful candy making. Temperature readings may vary from day to day even with the best thermometer, so test your thermometer before each use. To test, place it in enough water to cover the ball of mercury. Bring water to a boil. Let water boil for several minutes or until mercury rises no higher. Read the temperature at eye level. If it reads 212°, cook candy to exact degrees that recipe instructs. If reading is higher, cook candy as many degrees higher as the thermometer reads over 212°. For example, if thermometer reads 214° instead of 212° (2 degrees too high) and your recipe calls for 236°, cook candy to 238° (2 degrees higher than 236°). If your thermometer reads low when tested, adjust accordingly. For example, if your thermometer reads 208° instead of 212° (4 degrees too low) and your recipe calls for 236°, cook candy to 232° (4 degrees lower than 236°).

Many recipes state that candy is to be cooked to hard ball, soft ball, crack or thread stage. These terms describe the consistency of a small amount of cooked syrup when it is dropped into cold water. Hard ball is about 245° to 250°, soft ball is about 240°, crack is about 290° to 300° and thread is about 230°. Consistent results can only be obtained by using a thermometer. An incorrect temperature reading could result in extremely hard candy or candy so soft it cannot be handled.

Nearly all candy cooking can be started on high heat. Candies containing basically sugar and water may be cooked on high the whole time. Candies containing milk, cream, milk products or nondairy creamer products may be started on high, but the heat should be gradually lowered as the mixture gets heavier, so in the final stages the candy is cooking on medium low.

Undercooked Candy

If candy is not cooked long enough, several things can be done. In some instances, dry fondant can be mixed with soft candy to make it firm. Melted chocolate (real milk, semisweet, or compound coatings, etc.) can be mixed with candy before it cools. When chocolate hardens, candy becomes firm. Candy can be cooled to thicken and then dipped in chocolate. If candy is so soft that it cannot be handled, line molds with chocolate, spoon candy into molds and cover with chocolate.

Overcooked Candy

When candy is overcooked, it can easily be saved, as long as it is not scorched. Keep candy cooking on the stove; carefully add ¼ to ½ cup water (or milk or whatever liquid is used in the recipe) to boiling candy. The temperature should drop a few degrees below desired temperature. Continue cooking until the proper temperature is reached and proceed with the recipe.

Ingredients

In many recipes, butter and margarine can be used interchangeably. As a rule of thumb, use butter when the flavor of the butter contributes to the taste of the candy, such as in toffee, and margarine when the taste is predominately another flavor, such as with peanut butter or chocolate.

Candy made with milk products will cook with a residue on the bottom of saucepan, so it must be stirred while cooking to prevent sticking and scorching. There is an exception: heavy cream or nondairy coffee creamer is often used in recipes instead of milk for a richer flavor. These products will not stick and do not need to be stirred. Heavy cream or nondairy products yield a better quality candy, as there is very little chance of the candy becoming granular.

Candies with a sugar, corn syrup and water base should be stirred well to mix sugar completely with liquid, covered with a lid and brought to a rolling boil. Remove lid, insert thermometer and cook candy to desired temperature without stirring. Covering candy the first few minutes of cooking prevents sugar crystals from forming on side of pan and eliminates the possibility of grainy candy. Use of a lid eliminates the need of washing down side of saucepan with a damp cloth as some recipes direct. Never use a lid, however, when preparing recipes calling for milk or cream or mixtures that might boil over.

Candy Basics

Pans

Candy can be cooked in a variety of pans. Heavier pans, such as those made of heavy aluminum, will give an even heat and help prevent scorching. When making candy with milk or cream, use a large heavy pan because milk will make candy cook up high. Do not stir candy unless specified in recipe as it may make candy grainy. This is especially true for fudges.

Most recipes can be doubled or tripled with no trouble as long as you have large pans. When doubling a recipe, you may need to increase the size of pan by three or four times in order to keep candy from boiling over, especially candy using milk or cream.

If candy does boil over, remove pan from heat and use a different burner to finish cooking candy or clean the burner. Candy will be less likely to boil over again if you pour it into a larger pan or wipe down side of pan with a damp cloth.

To Prevent Boilovers

Watch candy as it cooks and reduce heat if it threatens to boil over. This is especially important in recipes using cream or milk. Start such recipes on high heat, then turn down gradually to prevent boilover as well as scorching.

Chocolate

To many people, candy and chocolate are synonymous. To others, candy making with chocolate has been restricted to simple fudges, leaving hand-dipped chocolates to the professional candymaker. Today, however, with the use of flavored compound coatings, even the novice can prepare delicious, attractive chocolate candy. There are, however, a few simple guidelines to follow when using chocolate.

Chocolate and Compound Coatings

In this book, the word chocolate refers to real milk, semisweet or baking chocolate. Flavored compound coatings are specified as such. Either can make exceptionally good candy or waxy, poor quality candy, depending upon the ingredients used by the manufacturer. Either can be used interchangeably for dipping.

The main difference between real chocolate and compound coatings is the oil base used. Real milk chocolate is made from the cocoa bean by separating the cocoa butter from the powder, processing them separately and combining them again. Quality flavored compound coatings substitute coconut oil for the cocoa butter.

Real milk chocolate, as might be expected, is a higher quality product, more expensive and more difficult to handle. As compound coatings are easy to use, beginners may want to use them until they are more secure with candy-making methods; but chocolate lovers will eventually want to try real chocolate.

Amount of Chocolate to Melt for Dipping

The amount of chocolate needed to dip centers will vary. As a general rule, melt one pound of chocolate to coat one pound of centers (approximately 50 pieces). If centers are smaller than one-half-inch diameter or chocolate cooler than specified, more chocolate should be used. Conversely, if centers are larger than average or chocolate is warmer than specified, less chocolate per pound will be needed.

Melting Chocolate

Chocolate must be heated gently, always over hot, not boiling, water in a double boiler rather than over direct heat. Heat water in the bottom of double boiler, remove from heat, place chocolate in top of double boiler and stir to melt. It is important not to allow any water, steam, or milk to drip on chocolate. If you lift the top of the double boiler from the water, dry the base of the pan; should a drop of water fall in the chocolate, remove it with a spoon. One drop of water can cause chocolate to become grainy.

If chocolate does not melt properly, chances are it is either old or has been exposed to moisture. Stir a tablespoon or two of coconut oil or paramount crystals into chocolate. Vegetable oil can be substituted for coconut oil, but the result is not as flavorful.

Tempering Real Chocolate for Dipping

When dipping in real chocolate, tempering is necessary for a successful end result. Real chocolate that is not tempered properly will take a very long time to set up, and when firm, it will have bloom or white streaks and spots. If you think you have the chocolate properly tempered, dip one center into it, remove, place on waxed paper and wait a few minutes. If the chocolate was tempered properly, it will set within a few minutes. If it does not set within ten minutes or if it dries with bloom, you probably need to go through the tempering process again. Although the process of using real chocolate is somewhat lengthy, real chocolate lovers will agree that the results are worth the extra effort.

Tempering chocolate is simply melting, cooling, then bringing chocolate back to the proper dipping temperature. Tempering chocolate before dipping results in a shiny, firm surface for the final product. Real chocolate *must* be tempered; compound coatings can be tempered, but it is not necessary.

To temper chocolate properly, follow these steps:

1. Melt proper amount of chocolate and vegetable shortening in a small bowl set in a pan of very warm water. Make sure water level is 2 to 3 inches below rim of bowl. (Water temperature should not be above 120°F.)

2. Heat chocolate to 108°F, stirring constantly with rubber spatula; scrape down side and bottom of bowl frequently so that the chocolate is evenly and uniformly heated.

3. When chocolate reaches 108°F, remove bowl from pan of water. Stir frequently until chocolate cools to 85°F. Continue stirring and scraping bowl constantly until chocolate cools to 80°F.

4. Keep chocolate at 80°F, stirring constantly, for 10 minutes. This is important because it develops the crystals necessary for gloss, It may be necessary to briefly set bowl in warm water to maintain temperature.

5. Rewarm chocolate in pan of warm water to 86°F; hold at that temperature for 5 minutes before dipping.

6. *Important:* Keep chocolate at 86°F during entire dipping process. If temperature at this point goes below 84°F, the entire tempering process must be repeated from Step 2.

7. Centers must be room temperature before dipping. (Dipping chilled centers may result in cracked surface and/or bloom.)

8. Dip room temperature centers or confections completely in tempered, melted chocolate. Dip one at a time using fork, fondue fork, or hat pin. Gently tap fork on side of bowl to remove excess chocolate. Invert onto waxed paper-covered tray; swirl small amount of coating over utensil marks.

9. Candies may be chilled a maximum of 15 minutes in refrigerator to help surface harden. Remove promptly or bloom may occur.

10. Store candies at room temperature (60°-75°F); keep them well covered.

Basic equipment for candy making.

Melted chocolate.

Thickened tempered chocolate ready to reheat.

Candy Basics

Preparing Chocolate for Dipping Without Breaking the Temper

Real chocolate comes from the manufacturer in perfect temper. Therefore, if you can melt the chocolate without breaking the temper, the process is much quicker and the results are more likely to be acceptable. Here are two methods:

1. Chop chocolate finely and heat over 95° water until chocolate is melted but still contains softened chunks. Remove from water; continue stirring rapidly until chocolate is smooth and free of lumps. Chocolate temperature should be 86 to 89°F. It is now ready for dipping or molding.

2. Chop the chocolate finely and melt ¾ of the amount over 95° water. When melted and smooth, remove from water and add remaining finely chopped chocolate. Stir until completely smooth and at a temperature of 86 to 89°F. It is now ready for dipping or molding.

Melting Coatings for Dipping

To prepare flavored compound coatings for dipping, follow these easy steps:

1. Heat water to a boil in bottom of double boiler.

2. Remove water from heat; place compound coating in top of double boiler.

3. Stir occasionally until compound coating is melted (about 3 to 5 minutes).

4. Remove top of double boiler from hot water and allow compound coating to cool for 10 to 20 minutes; or place over cold water and stir until thickened slightly.

5. Replace hot water with warm water in bottom of double boiler.

6. When compound coating has thickened slightly, place it over warm water and begin dipping centers. If it is too thick for dipping, warm water slightly. If compound coating is too thin, replace water with cooler water. Keep compound coating stirred while dipping.

Temperatures for Dipping

Real Milk Chocolate	86°
Real Semisweet Chocolate	90°
Compound Coatings	98°

Dipping Centers

Successful dipping is largely dependent upon three factors: using a quality real chocolate or compound coating, having the correct temperature and consistency, and stirring thoroughly.

The temperature of the room is as important as that of the chocolate or compound coating. The room should be between 60° and 70°, and results are best on a clear, cool day. When dipping, keep chocolate or compound coating over tepid water, at the temperature specified under "Temperatures for Dipping."

While dipping centers in chocolate, continue stirring chocolate rapidly with a circular motion. This results in proper blending of cocoa butter and ensures a rich, glossy coating.

Roll fondant balls for dipping.

Dip fondant.

Chocolate-covered fondant candies.

Chocolate Box with hand-molded chocolate roses, filled with cornstarch molded creams.

Easy Candy

Pecan Caramel Chews

Makes approximately 20.

  ½ pound caramel, purchased or homemade
1¼ cups pecan pieces or halves
1½ pounds real milk chocolate, melted for dipping

Melt caramel in heavy saucepan over low heat. Spread a solid layer of pecans on buttered cookie sheet. Drizzle melted caramel on pecans; chill until caramel hardens. Break caramel-nut mixture into pieces. Completely dip candy in melted chocolate or just cover caramel portion.

Peanut Fudge Bars

Makes approximately 25.

  1 4-ounce package noninstant chocolate pudding mix
  1 cup granulated sugar
  ½ cup frozen nondairy coffee creamer, thawed
  2 tablespoons butter
  ¾ cup chopped salted peanuts
  ½ teaspoon vanilla

Combine pudding mix, sugar, creamer and butter in small saucepan; cook to 235° on a candy thermometer. Remove from heat; stir in nuts and vanilla. Beat until mixture begins to thicken. Spread quickly in 8-inch square pan. Cut into bars while still warm.

Heath Crunch Candy

Makes 1 pound.

  1 pound chocolate-flavored compound coating (any type)*
  ½ cup Heath crunches (any flavor)*

Melt chocolate-flavored compound coating in double boiler over hot water; add crunch. Drop mixture into paper candy cups or drop in clusters on waxed paper. For bark, spread mixture out on waxed paper. Place another sheet of waxed paper on top; roll with rolling pin to thin candy. Let set; break into pieces.

*Note: Use crunch that will blend well with desired compound coating. For example: Peppermint crunch with white compound coating, lemon crunch with yellow compound coating, toffee or pecan-crisp crunch with sweet chocolate-flavored coating or cinnamon crunch with pink compound coating.

Peanut Butter Sandwiches

Makes approximately 80.

  2 pounds real sweet chocolate
  ¼ cup corn oil
  1 pound butterscotch compound coating, wafers or pieces
  1 cup peanut butter

Melt sweet chocolate and corn oil together in double boiler over hot water. Pour half of mixture in waxed paper-lined 9 x 13-inch pan. Cool until almost set. Keep remaining chocolate mixture warm over hot water. Melt butterscotch compound coating in double boiler over hot water; add peanut butter; blend well. Spread butterscotch mixture over chocolate layer. Cool until almost set. Pour remaining chocolate mixture over butterscotch layer. Cool until set; cut into small bars.

Maple Nut Bars

Makes approximately 80.

  2 pounds milk chocolate-flavored compound coating
  4 tablespoons vegetable oil
1½ pounds butterscotch compound coating, wafers or pieces
  1 cup chopped walnuts
  2 tablespoons maple flavoring

Melt chocolate-flavored compound coating in double boiler over hot water. Blend in 1 tablespoon vegetable oil; pour into waxed paper-lined 12 x 18-inch pan. Cool. Melt butterscotch compound coating in double boiler over hot water; add remaining vegetable oil, nuts and maple flavoring. Blend well. Pour quickly over first layer. Cut into bars when cool.

Raisin Clusters

Makes approximately 20.

1½ cups finely chopped real milk chocolate
1 cup finely chopped real semisweet chocolate
½ cup sweetened condensed milk
¼ cup marshmallow creme
½ teaspoon vanilla
1 cup raisins
½ cup nuts

Melt chocolates together in double boiler over hot water. Add condensed milk, marshmallow creme and vanilla; beat until smooth. Stir in raisins and nuts. Drop by spoonfuls in clusters on waxed paper. When set, store in covered container.

Note: Compounds may be used instead of real chocolate, if desired. Also all milk chocolate or all semisweet chocolate or any combination of the two may be used.

Butterscotch Nut Log

Makes 1.

1⅓ cups butterscotch compound coating, wafers *or* pieces
⅓ cup sweetened condensed milk
½ teaspoon vanilla
½ cup chopped pecans
    Pecan halves *or* large pieces

Melt butterscotch compound coating in double boiler over hot water. Add milk and vanilla; blend well. Stir in chopped pecans. Form into log 1-inch in diameter. Roll and wrap tightly in waxed paper to keep its shape; chill until firm. Remove paper. Press pecan halves into roll. Slice to serve.

Candy Cookies

Makes approximately 30.

1 cup blanched salted peanuts
2 cups Captain Crunch cereal
2 cups tinted miniature marshmallows
1 pound white compound coating

Combine peanuts, cereal and marshmallows in large bowl. Melt compound coating in double boiler over hot water. Cool slightly; pour over cereal mixture. Stir well to coat evenly. Drop by spoonfuls onto waxed paper.

Candy Hash

Makes approximately 30 pieces.

1 pound white compound coating
1¼ cups salted peanuts
2½ cups broken pretzel sticks

Melt compound coating in double boiler over hot water; blend in peanuts and pretzels until well coated. Spread in a thin layer on waxed paper. When cool and set, break into pieces.

Crispy Fudge Sandwiches

Makes approximately 25.

1 cup butterscotch compound coating, wafers *or* pieces
½ cup extra crunchy peanut butter
1 cup miniature marshmallows
4 cups crisp rice cereal
1 cup semisweet chocolate-flavored compound coating, wafers *or* pieces
1 tablespoon paramount crystals *or* corn oil
2 tablespoons marshmallow creme
¼ cup confectioners' sugar
2 tablespoons butter

Melt butterscotch compound coating in double boiler over hot water. Add peanut butter, marshmallows and cereal. With dampened hands press one-half mixture in bottom of 8-inch square pan. Melt semisweet chocolate-flavored compound coating and paramount crystals in double boiler over hot water. Add remaining ingredients; beat until smooth and well blended. Drop fudge mixture by spoonfuls over cereal mixture; smooth with dampened fingers. Spread remaining cereal mixture over fudge. Chill until firm; cut into squares.

Marshmallow Cups

Makes approximately 32.

>   1 pound real semisweet *or* sweet chocolate,
>   for dipping
>   2 cups marshmallow creme

Melt chocolate in double boiler over hot water. Line medium-size candy cups with melted chocolate using a good quality brush; chill in freezer. Remove from freezer; fill chocolate cup with marshmallow creme to within 1/16 inch of top.* Completely seal top with additional melted chocolate, starting at outside rim in circular motion and finishing in center. Chill; wrap in foil.

Variation

Peanut Butter Cups: Substitute 2 cups peanut butter for marshmallow creme.

Note: For easy filling, pipe filling into cups using a pastry bag fitted with a coupling.

Cheesy Coconut Easter Eggs

Makes approximately 40.

>   1 3-ounce package cream cheese, softened
>   1/2 teaspoon vanilla
>   1 pound (approximately) confectioners' sugar
>   1/4 cup flaked coconut
>   Dash salt
>   1 pound (approximately) chocolate-flavored *or*
>   pastel compound coating, melted

Combine cream cheese and vanilla in bowl. Gradually add confectioners' sugar, coconut and salt. Mix to consistency that can be easily handled, adding more confectioners' sugar if necessary. Form candy into eggs; let set approximately 1 hour. Dip into compound coating; let set until firm.

Peanut Butter-Marshmallow Eggs

Makes approximately 80.

>   1 1/2 cups butter *or* margarine, softened
>   5 to 6 cups sifted confectioners' sugar
>   1 cup peanut butter
>   1 3/4 cups marshmallow creme
>   2 teaspoons vanilla
>   1 3/4 pounds (approximately) real milk chocolate,
>   melted for dipping

Cream butter and 2 cups confectioners' sugar in large bowl until light and fluffy. Add peanut butter, marshmallow creme and vanilla; blend well. Gradually add remaining confectioners' sugar; mix to consistency that can be easily handled. Form into egg shapes. Dip eggs in melted chocolate; let stand until firm.

Easy No-Cook Fondant

Makes approximately 80 centers.

>   1/2 cup butter *or* margarine, room temperature
>   2 1-pound boxes confectioners' sugar
>   1 13 1/4-ounce can sweetened condensed milk
>   1 teaspoon vanilla *or* other flavoring
>   1/4 teaspoon salt
>   Nuts, coconut *or* chopped candied fruit, optional
>   Food coloring, optional
>   1 3/4 pounds (approximately) real milk chocolate,
>   melted for dipping

Combine butter, 1 pound confectioners' sugar and condensed milk in large bowl; add vanilla and salt. Gradually add remaining sugar, first with spoon and then knead by hand. Add nuts, coconut or candied fruit and food coloring, if desired. Form mixture into small balls; let stand a few hours and dip in melted chocolate.

Layered Mints

Makes approximately 100.

>   3 pounds white compound coating
>   2 tablespoons vegetable oil
>   1 1/2 pounds light green compound coating, wafers *or*
>   pieces
>   1/2 teaspoon peppermint oil
>   1/2 teaspoon vanilla butternut oil

Melt white compound coating and vegetable oil together in double boiler over hot water. Pour half of mixture in waxed paper-lined 12 x 18-inch pan; keep remaining mixture over hot water. Melt green compound coating in double boiler over hot water. Blend in remaining oils. Pour over white compound coating in pan; let set. Pour remaining white compound coating mixture over green. Cut into squares when cool.

*Top Left: Marble Fudge, page 13; Coconut Fudge, page 13.
Top Right: Pecan Caramel Chews, page 8.
Center: Crispy Fudge Sandwiches, page 9.
Bottom Left, from Top: Toffee Bark, Peppermint Bark, Almond Bark, Cinnamon Bark, all page 8, using basic Heath Crunch Candy.
Bottom Right: Cherry Coconut Creams, page 12.*

Easy Candy

Cherry Coconut Creams

Makes 36.

- 1 cup semisweet chocolate-flavored compound coating, wafers *or* pieces
- 1/3 cup frozen nondairy coffee creamer, thawed
- 1/8 teaspoon salt
- 1 1/2 cups confectioners' sugar
- 1/4 teaspoon almond flavoring
- 1/2 teaspoon vanilla
- 3/4 cup walnut pieces
- 1/2 cup coarsely chopped maraschino cherries, well drained
- 1 1/4 cups toasted *or* desiccated coconut

Heat chocolate-flavored compound coating, creamer and salt in double boiler over hot water until compound coating is melted; stir until smooth. Add confectioners' sugar; blend well. Add flavorings, nuts and cherries. Chill until firm enough to handle. Form into 1-inch balls; roll in coconut.

Cherry Popcorn

Makes 30 pieces.

- 1 3-ounce package cherry-flavored gelatin *or* any flavor desired
- 1 cup granulated sugar
- 1 cup light corn syrup
- 1/4 teaspoon salt
- 1 tablespoon butter
- 7 quarts popped corn
- 1 cup blanched roasted peanuts
- 1 1/2 cups semisweet chocolate-flavored compound coating, wafers *or* pieces, melted, optional

Combine gelatin, sugar, corn syrup, salt and butter in large 8-quart pan. Bring to full rolling boil, stirring constantly. Remove from heat; add popped corn and peanuts. Stir until well coated with syrup mixture. Pour onto well-buttered 10 x 15-inch cookie sheet. When cool drizzle chocolate-flavored compound coating over Popcorn, if desired. Cut into squares; wrap each square in plastic wrap.

Peanut Butter Crispy Bars

Makes approximately 80.

- 1 1/2 pounds peanut butter compound coating, wafers *or* pieces
- 1 cup peanut butter
- 5 cups crisp rice cereal
- 2 pounds sweet chocolate-flavored compound coating, melted

Melt peanut butter compound coating in double boiler over hot water; blend in peanut butter. Fold in cereal; spread in waxed paper-lined 12 x 18-inch pan. When set, cut into bars and dip in chocolate-flavored compound coating.

Pink Cinnamon Crunch

Makes approximately 50 pieces.

- 1 pound pink compound coating
- 1 cup Heath cinnamon crunch
- 1 1/2 cups crisp rice cereal
- Real semisweet chocolate, melted

Melt compound coating in double boiler over hot water; stir in cinnamon crunch and cereal. Spread mixture on waxed paper. Drizzle with chocolate. Let set; break into pieces.

Cathedral Candies

Makes approximately 45 pieces.

- 2 1/2 cups white compound coating, wafers *or* pieces
- 1/4 teaspoon salt
- 1/2 cup butter *or* margarine, melted
- 2 eggs
- 1 cup chopped nuts
- 1 10 1/2-ounce package tinted miniature marshmallows
- 1 teaspoon vanilla
- 2 1/2 cups (approximately) confectioners' sugar

Melt compound coating in double boiler over hot water; add salt and butter. Add eggs one at a time while compound coating mixture is still over hot water; beat well after each addition. Add nuts, marshmallows and vanilla; blend well. Sprinkle confectioners' sugar over three 10 x 12-inch pieces of foil. Pour candy onto sugar-covered foil; form into 3 rolls about 2 inches in diameter. Coat each roll with sugar. Wrap tightly in foil. Refrigerate and slice as needed.

Choco-Peanut Butter Fudge

Makes approximately 25 pieces.

    2 cups melted real milk chocolate
    ⅔ cup smooth peanut butter
    1 tablespoon honey
    2 tablespoons light corn syrup

Combine all ingredients; beat until smooth. Spread in 7-inch square pan. Cut into pieces when set.

Coconut Fudge

Makes approximately 50 pieces.

    Toasted flaked coconut
    1 pound white compound coating
    ¾ cup marshmallow creme
    ⅔ cup sweetened condensed milk or
      ½ cup plus 1 tablespoon Homemade Sweetened
      Condensed Milk (Recipe on page 37)
    ½ cup desiccated coconut
    ½ cup chopped nuts

Line a 7-inch square pan with double layers of foil; butter foil. Sprinkle toasted coconut generously over bottom of pan; set aside. Melt white compound coating in double boiler over hot water. Add marshmallow creme, sweetened condensed milk, coconut and nuts; blend well. Carefully spread mixture in prepared pan; keep coconut from mixing into fudge. Sprinkle a generous amount of toasted coconut on top of fudge; press in. Let cool several hours; cut into squares.

Marble Fudge

Makes approximately 50 pieces.

    1 pound white compound coating
    ⅔ cup sweetened condensed milk or
      ½ cup plus 1 tablespoon Homemade Sweetened
      Condensed Milk (Recipe on page 37)
    ¾ cup marshmallow creme
    ½ cup chopped nuts
    ¾ cup confetti chips (light chocolate, semisweet
      chocolate or any color combination)
    1 pound real milk chocolate, melted for dipping,
      optional

Line a 7-inch square pan with double layers of foil; butter foil. Melt white compound coating in double boiler over hot water; add milk, marshmallow creme and nuts. Blend well. Add confetti chips; stir quickly. *Do not* let chips melt com-

pletely. Spread immediately in prepared pan. Let cool several hours; cut into squares. Candy may be dipped in melted chocolate, if desired.

Fruit Nut Fudge

Makes approximately 50 pieces.

    1¾ cups granulated sugar
    ⅔ cup frozen nondairy coffee creamer, thawed
    ⅛ teaspoon salt
    1¼ cups finely chopped real semisweet chocolate
    1½ cups miniature marshmallows
    1 teaspoon vanilla
    4 tablespoons butter
    ⅛ teaspoon cinnamon
    ½ cup coarsely chopped candied cherries and
      pineapple
    ½ cup coarsely chopped walnuts

Combine sugar, creamer and salt in heavy saucepan; cook to 238° on a candy thermometer. Remove from heat. Add chocolate and marshmallows to hot mixture; blend well. Add vanilla, butter and cinnamon. Fold in fruit and nuts; pour into 8-inch square pan. Cut into squares when firm.

Easy Pecan Rolls

Makes 8.

    1 7½-ounce jar marshmallow creme
    1 1-pound box confectioners' sugar
    1 teaspoon vanilla
    ¼ teaspoon butter flavoring
    1 pound caramel, purchased or homemade
    1 to 2 tablespoons cream or half-and-half, optional
    4 cups (approximately) chopped pecans

Combine marshmallow creme, sugar and flavorings, kneading until sugar is absorbed completely. Shape into 8 rolls. Wrap each roll in plastic wrap and freeze. Melt caramel in double boiler over hot water; keep warm. If caramel is too thick for dipping, add 1 to 2 tablespoons cream. Dip each roll in caramel; roll immediately in chopped pecans. Wrap tightly and store in a cool place.

Caramels

Makes approximately 50.

- 1 14-ounce can sweetened condensed milk
- 1 cup light corn syrup
- ½ teaspoon salt
- 1 teaspoon vanilla
- 1 tablespoon butter
- 1 pound real milk chocolate, melted for dipping, optional

Combine milk and syrup in heavy 2-quart saucepan. Cook, stirring constantly, to 240 - 245° on a candy thermometer (cook longer for a firmer caramel). Remove from heat and add salt, vanilla and butter; blend well. Pour into buttered 8-inch square pan. Cut into squares when cool. Dip in melted chocolate, if desired, or wrap in plastic wrap.

Note: This recipe can be used in other recipes that require caramel.

Peanut Butter Caramels

Makes approximately 60.

- ½ cup chopped peanuts *or* pecans
- ½ cup smooth peanut butter
- 2½ cups granulated sugar
- ¾ cup light corn syrup
- 6 tablespoons butter
- ⅛ teaspoon salt
- ½ teaspoon lecithin, optional
- 2 cups whipping cream

Butter a 9-inch square pan. Sprinkle nuts over bottom of pan. Combine remaining ingredients except 1 cup cream in heavy 3-quart saucepan. Bring to boil over medium heat, stirring constantly. Gradually add remaining 1 cup cream when mixture is at a full rolling boil. Continue to stir, lowering heat as mixture thickens. Cook to 245° on a candy thermometer; pour over nuts. Cool. When firm cut into squares and wrap.

Soft Caramels

Makes approximately 80.

- 2 cups granulated sugar
- 1½ cups light corn syrup
- 2 cups whipping cream
- ¼ cup butter, cut into small pieces
- 1 teaspoon vanilla

Combine sugar, corn syrup and ¼ cup whipping cream in heavy 2½-quart saucepan; cook to 238° on a candy thermometer; stir only to dissolve sugar. Add an additional ¼ cup whipping cream slowly so boiling does not stop. Heat again to 238°. Add remaining 1½ cups whipping cream slowly so boiling does not stop; cook to 240° keeping on medium heat so mixture does not scorch. Stir only as necessary. Remove from heat; add butter and vanilla. Stir gently until butter is melted and blended. Pour into a buttered 9-inch square pan for thick caramels or a 9 x 13-inch pan for thin caramels.

Almond Caramels

Makes approximately 100.

- 2½ cups light corn syrup
- 1 cup invert sugar
- 1½ cups granulated sugar
- 1 14-ounce can sweetened condensed milk
- ½ cup butter
- 1 pound toasted almonds, slivered *or* pieces
- 2 pounds real milk chocolate, melted for dipping, optional

Combine corn syrup, sugars, condensed milk and butter in heavy saucepan; cook to 245° on a candy thermometer, stirring constantly. Pour mixture into two buttered 8-inch square pans; press almonds into top; set aside to cool. When cool, cut into squares. Wrap in plastic wrap or, if desired, dip caramels three-quarters of the way into chocolate so nuts show on top.

Variation

Maple Caramels: Substitute 2 teaspoons maple flavoring for the toasted almonds.

Clockwise, from Top: Chocolate Easter Eggs, page 25; Easter Egg Candies, page 25; Choco-Peanut Butter Easter Eggs, page 25 and Cheesy Coconut Easter Eggs, page 11, surrounded by Peanut Butter-Marshmallow Eggs, page 11.

Candy and Candy Molding Cookbook 15

Caramels & Mints

Evaporated Milk Caramels

Makes approximately 100.

5 cups granulated sugar
1½ cups light corn syrup
1 cup butter
1 teaspoon cream of tartar
2 cups evaporated milk
2 cups chopped walnuts
¼ teaspoon salt

Combine sugar, syrup, butter, cream of tartar and 1 cup milk in large heavy saucepan. Stir and bring to rolling boil. Add remaining milk slowly so boiling does not stop. Continue cooking and stirring to 245-250° on a candy thermometer. Remove from heat and add nuts and salt; blend well. Pour into a buttered 9 x 13-inch pan. Cool and cut into squares.

Note: Cooking to 250° produces a very firm caramel.

Penny's Time-Saving Caramels

Makes approximately 50 to 80.

1 cup butter
1 1-pound box light brown sugar
⅛ teaspoon salt
1 cup light corn syrup
1 14-ounce can sweetened condensed milk
1 teaspoon vanilla

Melt butter in heavy 3-quart saucepan; stir in sugar and salt; bring to a boil. Add syrup; blend well and return to a boil. Add milk, stirring constantly; cook to 245° on a candy thermometer. Continue to stir constantly; lower heat as mixture thickens. Remove from heat and stir in vanilla. Pour into a buttered 9-inch square pan. Cool; cut into squares and wrap.

Variation

Chocolate Caramels: Prepare Penny's Caramels as directed in recipe. After adding milk, cook to 235° and add 5-ounces melted baking chocolate. Continue cooking to 245°.

Orange Caramels

Makes approximately 64.

2 cups granulated sugar
Dash salt
2 cups light corn syrup
1 6-ounce can frozen orange juice concentrate
½ cup butter
1 cup whipping cream

Combine sugar, salt, corn syrup and orange juice concentrate in heavy saucepan; cook to 245° on a candy thermometer, stirring occasionally. Add butter and cream slowly so boiling does not stop. Cook to 252°; continue to stir occasionally. Pour into well-buttered 9-inch square pan. Chill. Cut into squares when cold.

Layered Caramels

Makes approximately 100 to 140.

1 recipe Penny's Time-Saving Caramels (Recipe on this page)
1 recipe Chocolate Caramels Variation (Recipe on this page)

Prepare Penny's Caramels according to recipe and pour into a buttered 9 x 13-inch pan. Let set 1 hour or until slightly warm to touch. Prepare Chocolate Caramels according to recipe; pour over plain caramels. Do not let first layer cool completely before adding second layer or layers will not adhere together.

Chewy Candy

Makes approximately 100 pieces.

2 cups granulated sugar
2 cups light corn syrup
1 cup whipping cream
½ cup butter
1 teaspoon salt
1 cup broken walnuts *or* pecans
1 teaspoon vanilla

Blend all ingredients except nuts and vanilla in 4-quart saucepan. Cook to 245° on a candy thermometer, stirring occasionally. Add nuts and vanilla; pour into buttered 10½ x 15-inch jelly-roll pan. Cool; cut into squares and wrap.

Chocolate Caramels from Purchased Caramel

Makes approximately 30.

> 1 pound purchased block caramel
> ½ cup finely chopped real semisweet chocolate

Melt caramel in microwave oven or over low heat in heavy saucepan. Add chocolate; blend until melted. Pour into buttered 6-inch square pan. Cut into squares when cool.

Layered Butterscotch

Makes approximately 36 pieces.

> 1 cup firmly packed light brown sugar
> 2 tablespoons light corn syrup
> ⅓ cup frozen nondairy coffee creamer, thawed
> ⅛ teaspoon salt
> 2 tablespoons butter
> 1 teaspoon vanilla

Combine sugar, syrup, creamer, salt and 1 tablespoon butter in heavy saucepan; cook to 240° on a candy thermometer. Add remaining butter and stir to dissolve; cook to 248°. Add vanilla; pour into buttered foil-lined 6-inch square pan.

Top and bottom layer:

> 1½ cups white compound coating
> 1 tablespoon paramount crystals *or* corn oil
> ½ cup finely chopped nuts

Melt compound coating in double boiler over hot water; add paramount crystals and blend well. Cool partially. Spread half of mixture over butterscotch layer. Let set. Keep remaining mixture warm over hot water. When compound coating layer has set, carefully peel foil away from butterscotch. Turn candy butterscotch-side up on clean piece of foil. Bring foil up around sides of candy to form frame. Spread remaining compound coating mixture over butterscotch; sprinkle with nuts. Let set. Cut into small squares; wrap in plastic wrap.

Cream Mints

Makes approximately 60.

> ½ cup water
> ¹⁄₁₆ teaspoon plain gelatin
> ¼ cup granulated sugar
> 1½ pounds Water Fondant, broken into pieces (Recipe on page 20)
> Flavoring
> Food coloring

Combine water and gelatin in heavy 1-quart saucepan. Heat over low heat until gelatin is dissolved. Add sugar; continue to heat, stirring until sugar is dissolved. Add fondant (in humid weather, add 1¾ pounds); heat to 155 - 160° on a candy thermometer. Add flavoring and food coloring as desired. Drop from spoon or candy funnel onto waxed paper. After tops dry, turn mints over to dry bottoms. Store when tops and bottoms are dry but insides are still creamy.

Party Mints

Makes approximately 150.

> ⅓ cup whipping cream
> ½ cup butter, melted
> 1 egg white
> ½ teaspoon cream of tartar
> Few grains salt
> Peppermint oil *or* any flavor oil
> Food coloring
> 2 1-pound boxes confectioners' sugar, sifted
> Granulated sugar, optional
> Real chocolate, melted for dipping, optional

Heat cream until hot but not boiling in 1-quart saucepan. Add butter, egg white, cream of tartar and salt. Add peppermint oil and food coloring*; blend well. Add confectioners' sugar, a small amount at a time, blending well after each addition with a spoon and then with hands. Add additional confectioners' sugar if necessary. Mints may be rolled in sugar and pressed into soft rubber molds, then immediately released, or may be formed into rolls and sliced or may be formed into patties. Let set to dry. Dip in melted chocolate, if desired.

*Note: If different flavors and/or colors are desired, divide finished candy and work in flavoring and food coloring after adding sugar.

Caramels & Mints

Mints

Makes approximately 50.

- 2 cups granulated sugar
- ½ cup water
- ½ cup light corn syrup
- 1 egg white
- ¼ teaspoon cream of tartar
  Flavoring
  Food coloring
  Confectioners' sugar

Combine sugar, water and corn syrup in heavy saucepan; cook to 275° on a candy thermometer. Beat egg white in small bowl; add cream of tartar and continue to beat until stiff. Pour cooked syrup mixture over beaten egg white; beat until firm, adding flavoring and food coloring. Pour out onto surface heavily dusted with confectioners' sugar. Knead with hands; form into long strands. Cut into small pieces.

Buttermints

Makes approximately 80.

- 1 cup water
- 3 cups granulated sugar
- 1½ tablespoons whipping cream
- 1½ teaspoons white vinegar
- ½ teaspoon salt
- 2 tablespoons butter
- 3 or 4 drops peppermint oil

Combine water, sugar, cream, vinegar, salt and butter in heavy saucepan; cook to 258° on a candy thermometer. Pour on cold buttered surface. Let cool slightly. Pull candy until it turns bright white and ridges form. Add peppermint oil as you pull candy. Pull out into a twisted rope; cut with scissors into bite-size pieces.

Cream Cheese Mints

Makes 30 to 50.

- 1 3-ounce package cream cheese, room temperature
  Few drops each desired food coloring and flavoring
- 2½ cups confectioners' sugar
  Granulated sugar

Combine cream cheese with food coloring and flavoring in bowl. Work in confectioners' sugar, first with spoon and then knead with hands to form doughlike mixture. Roll in balls; dip each in granulated sugar. Press into soft rubber molds and immediately release. Let mints form a crust; store in covered container.

Compound Chocolate Mints

Makes 75 to 100.

- 1½ pounds compound coating, wafers or pieces, any color
  Powdered food coloring, optional
  Few drops peppermint, wintergreen, orange or lemon oil, to taste

Melt compound coating in double boiler over hot water. *Do not* let water boil. Add food coloring, if desired. Stir gently until compound coating is smooth and melted; add oil. Fill mint molds. (Squeeze bottle can be used for ease and speed. Keep bottle in warm water when not in use so compound coating does not set.) *Do not* overfill molds. Tap molds gently on table to remove air bubbles. Chill in freezer 5 minutes. When set, turn mold over and gently tap mints out onto waxed paper.

Bavarian Mints

Makes 70 to 80.

- 1¼ pounds compound coating, sweet, semisweet or combination
- 4½ cups dry fondant
- 2½ tablespoons light corn syrup
- 1 cup evaporated milk or frozen nondairy coffee creamer, thawed
- ¼ teaspoon invertase
- ⅛ teaspoon peppermint oil

Melt compound coating in double boiler over hot water. Combine remaining ingredients in mixing bowl; beat 10 to 12 minutes at low speed. Gradually add melted compound coating to fondant mixture at medium speed. Blend well; beat at high speed ½ minute; spread in buttered 10 x 15-inch pan. Cut into squares when set.

Note: Real chocolate may be substituted for compound coating.

Top, from Left: Almond Caramels, page 15; Peanut Butter Caramels, page 15; Layered Butterscotch, page 17. Bottom Left: Variations of Party Mints, page 17. Bottom Right: Buttermints, page 18.

Fondants

Basic Fondant

Makes approximately 100 centers.

- 5 cups granulated sugar
- 1 cup frozen nondairy coffee creamer, thawed
- 1 cup whipping cream
- ¼ cup butter *or* margarine
- ½ teaspoon cream of tartar
  Flavoring
  Food coloring

Combine all ingredients, except flavoring and food coloring, in large saucepan. Stir until sugar is moistened. Start to cook on high and gradually lower heat as mixture thickens. Cook to 237° on a candy thermometer. Pour onto cold surface; cool slightly. Work with fondant paddle until firm; knead with hands until smooth. Add flavoring and food coloring as desired.

Note: Great for peppermint patties *or* any fruit-flavored cream center.

Water Fondant

Makes approximately 40 centers.

- 2 cups granulated sugar
  Dash salt
- 2 tablespoons light corn syrup
- ¾ cup boiling water
- ½ teaspoon vanilla

Combine all ingredients, except vanilla, in small saucepan; blend well. Cover with tight fitting lid; cook until steam comes from under lid. Remove lid, insert a candy thermometer and cook to 240° without stirring. Immediately pour fondant onto cold surface; cool slightly. Work with spatula until fondant is white and creamy. Add vanilla; knead until well blended. Let stand, uncovered, until cold. Wrap in plastic wrap until ready to use.

Note: If fondant sets hard as you work, immediately break off small pieces and work in palms of hands until soft and creamy. Set each piece aside; blend all softened pieces together and wrap in plastic wrap. (Fondant stays soft if wrapped.)

Water Fondant Fruit Centers

Makes approximately 40.

- 2 cups prepared Water Fondant (Recipe on page 20)
- 2 tablespoons fruit preserves
- 1 teaspoon lemon juice
- 2 drops food coloring
  All-purpose flour
- 1 pound (approximately) real milk chocolate, melted for dipping

Divide fondant in half. Blend 1 tablespoon preserves into each half; add ½ teaspoon lemon juice and 1 drop coloring to each half. Work with fondant paddle until all ingredients are well blended. Let set, uncovered, until firm. Form fondant into centers. Dust hands frequently with flour to prevent sticking. When centers are dry on top, turn them over to dry bottoms. Dip in melted chocolate.

Rich Butter Fondant

Makes approximately 60 centers.

- 2¼ cups granulated sugar
- ¼ cup invert sugar
- ½ cup milk
- ½ cup whipping cream
- ⅛ teaspoon salt
- ¼ cup butter
- ½ teaspoon cream of tartar
- 1 teaspoon vanilla
  Flavoring, optional
- ½ cup finely chopped nuts, optional
- 1¼ pounds (approximately) real milk chocolate, melted for dipping

Combine first seven ingredients in 2½-quart saucepan. Cook with minimum of stirring to 240° on a candy thermometer. Gradually lower heat as mixture thickens. Pour onto cold surface; cool slightly. Work with spatula until thick and creamy; add vanilla as you work. Add flavoring and nuts, if desired. Let candy rest 1 hour; form into balls and dip in melted chocolate.

Peanut Butter Fondant

Makes approximately 30 centers.

    1¼ cups granulated sugar
    ⅔ cup whipping cream
    1 tablespoon light corn syrup
    ⅛ teaspoon salt
    ⅓ cup miniature marshmallows
    1 teaspoon vanilla
    ¼ cup peanut butter
    ¾ pound (approximately) real milk chocolate,
      melted for dipping

Combine sugar, cream, corn syrup and salt in small heavy saucepan; cook to 238° on a candy thermometer. Add marshmallows *(do not stir)*; pour onto marble slab. When slightly cooled, work vanilla in with spatula. When mixture begins to set, work in peanut butter. Continue to work until creamy. Let rest 1 hour. Roll into balls; dip in melted chocolate.

Double Butter Creamy Centers

Makes approximately 90.

    4 cups granulated sugar
    2½ cups frozen nondairy coffee creamer, thawed
    1 cup light corn syrup
    ¼ teaspoon cream of tartar
    1 cup butter *or* margarine, softened
    ⅛ teaspoon baking soda
    1 teaspoon vanilla
    4 drops butter flavoring, optional
    Nuts, optional

Cook sugar, creamer, corn syrup and cream of tartar to 225° on a candy thermometer in heavy saucepan; stir only until sugar is dissolved. Add ½ cup butter slowly so boiling does not stop; continue cooking to 238°. Pour out onto marble slab or other cool surface. When slightly cooled, work with fondant paddle, adding baking soda and vanilla. (If using margarine, add butter flavoring.) When fondant sets, work in remaining butter. Add additional flavoring and nuts, if desired. If fondant has not set in 10 minutes, spread on platter and rewarm in microwave or on cookie sheet in warm oven. *(Do not* let candy get hot, just slightly warm.) Return to slab; continue to work. Fondant can be rewarmed more than once, if necessary.

Caramel Creams

Makes approximately 80 centers.

    4½ cups granulated sugar
    ½ cup hot water
    1 cup whipping cream
    1 cup frozen nondairy coffee creamer, thawed
    ¼ cup light corn syrup
    ¼ teaspoon salt
    1 cup nuts, optional
    1 teaspoon vanilla
    1¾ pounds (approximately) real milk chocolate,
      melted for dipping

Melt ½ cup sugar in heavy saucepan. Add hot water; boil until sugar is dissolved. Add remaining 4 cups sugar, cream, creamer, corn syrup and salt. Cook without stirring to 238° on a candy thermometer. Cool slightly; work candy with spatula until creamy and firm. Add nuts, if desired. Add vanilla; work in. Shape into balls; dip in melted chocolate.

Strawberry Orientals

Makes approximately 75 centers.

    3 cups granulated sugar
    1 cup hot water
    ¼ cup pureed strawberries, frozen *or* fresh
    2 teaspoons glycerine
    ⅛ teaspoon salt
    1 egg white
    1 drop lemon flavoring
    1½ pounds (approximately) real milk chocolate,
      melted for dipping

Combine sugar, water, strawberries, glycerine and salt in 2½-quart saucepan. Blend well, cover tightly and boil until steam comes from under lid. Remove lid and insert candy thermometer; *do not stir*. When temperature reaches 235°, beat egg white at medium speed in small mixing bowl. At 242° remove syrup mixture from stove. If room is cold, warm marble slab slightly by placing hot pan on surface of slab. Pour mixture onto slab. Beat egg white on high 1 minute; spread over syrup mixture. Immediately work together until creamy and firm; add lemon flavoring as you work. Form immediately into balls; dip into melted chocolate as soon as possible so centers do not become dry.

Fondants

Cherry Creams

Makes 40 to 50 centers.

¾ pound (2 cups) finely chopped white
    compound coating
½ cup marshmallow creme
¼ cup cherry preserves
⅛ teaspoon concentrated cherry flavoring
¼ teaspoon almond flavoring
    Few drops red food coloring
1 pound (approximately) real milk chocolate,
    melted for dipping

Melt white compound coating in double boiler
over hot water. Add marshmallow creme, preserves, flavorings and food coloring all at once;
blend well. Let set in cool place 30 minutes or
until firm enough to form into balls. Dip in melted
chocolate.

Apricot Creams

Makes approximately 40.

2 cups granulated sugar
1 cup whipping cream
1 teaspoon light corn syrup
¾ cup finely chopped dried apricots
1 pound (approximately) real milk chocolate,
    melted for dipping

Combine sugar, cream and corn syrup in heavy
saucepan; cook to 230° on a candy thermometer. Add apricots; continue cooking to 234°, stirring gently so apricots do not scorch. Pour onto
cold surface. Cool slightly; work with spatula
until mixture sets. Roll into balls; dip in melted
chocolate.

French Chocolates

Makes approximately 50.

1 pound real milk chocolate, finely chopped
⅓ cup invert sugar
4½ tablespoons water
1 pound (approximately) real milk chocolate,
    melted for dipping
2 cups finely chopped nuts

Melt 1 pound milk chocolate in double boiler over
hot water; cool to 90° on a candy thermometer.
Meanwhile, heat invert sugar to 180°; cool to
100° and add water. Gradually add sugar-water
mixture to 90° chocolate, beating rapidly. Spread
in shallow 9 x 13-inch pan. When firm enough to

handle, form into balls; dip in melted chocolate.
Roll in chopped nuts while chocolate is still soft.

Cocoa Mocha Creams

Makes 90 to 100.

1 cup frozen nondairy coffee creamer, thawed
½ cup whipping cream
¼ cup instant coffee crystals
5 cups granulated sugar
¼ cup butter
2 1-ounce squares baking chocolate, melted
1 teaspoon vanilla
2 drops invertase
2 pounds (approximately) real milk chocolate,
    melted for dipping

Combine creamer, whipping cream and coffee
crystals in saucepan; heat until coffee is dissolved. Add sugar, butter and baking chocolate;
stir well and cook to 238° on a candy thermometer. Pour onto cold surface; cool slightly. Work
with spatula until creamy; add vanilla and invertase as you work. Cool completely to set; form
into balls and dip in melted chocolate.

Almond Vanilla Buttercreams

Makes approximately 80.

4½ cups granulated sugar
⅓ cup invert sugar
½ cup water
1¼ cups whipping cream
½ teaspoon salt
1 teaspoon vanilla
2 drops invertase
1 cup marshmallow creme
½ pound chopped toasted almonds
1¾ pounds (approximately) real milk chocolate,
    melted for dipping

Cook sugars and water to rolling boil. Add whipping cream slowly; cook to 244° on a candy
thermometer. Pour onto cold surface. Cool partially and work with spatula. When fondant starts
to set, add salt, vanilla, invertase and marshmallow creme. Continue to work until fondant sets.
Add nuts, reserving some for decoration. Form
into balls; dip in melted chocolate. Decorate each
with a piece of almond while chocolate is still
soft.

Top Tier: Cherry Creams, this page; Chocolate Truffles, page 24.
Bottom Tier: Apricot Creams (in paper cups), this page;
Butterscotch Creams, page 25.
Tray: French Chocolates (with nuts), page 22;
Strawberry Orientals, page 21.

Fondants

Maple Syrup Creams

Makes approximately 40.

> 1 cup frozen nondairy coffee creamer, thawed
> 2 cups maple syrup
> 1 pound (approximately) real milk chocolate, melted for dipping

Cook creamer and syrup in heavy saucepan to 238° on a candy thermometer. Cool slightly on marble slab; work with spatula until candy holds its shape. Roll into balls; dip in melted milk chocolate.

Chocolate Truffles

Makes approximately 75.

> 1½ pounds real semisweet chocolate
> ¼ cup butter
> ¾ cup frozen nondairy coffee creamer, thawed
> ½ teaspoon vanilla
> 1½ pounds (approximately) real milk chocolate, melted for dipping
> 1 cup finely chopped real milk chocolate *or* ½ cup melted real milk chocolate, for decoration

Melt semisweet chocolate in double boiler over hot water. Heat butter, creamer and vanilla in separate saucepan to 125° on a candy thermometer. Add to semisweet chocolate all at once, beating until smooth and creamy. Chill in refrigerator until nearly set but still pliable. Beat with mixer until light and fluffy. Spread in buttered 9-inch square pan. Let set and cut into squares or return to refrigerator until set enough to roll into balls; dip in melted chocolate. Sprinkle generously with chopped chocolate or pipe melted chocolate from pastry bag in decorative design.

Mocha Truffles

Makes approximately 50.

> 1⅓ pounds real milk chocolate, finely chopped
> ⅔ cup half-and-half
> 2 tablespoons instant coffee crystals
> 1 teaspoon vanilla
> 1 pound (approximately) real milk chocolate, melted for dipping
> ½ cup finely shaved real semisweet chocolate

Melt 1⅓ pounds real milk chocolate in double boiler over hot water. Heat half-and-half to 130° on a candy thermometer in separate saucepan; stir in coffee crystals and vanilla. Add half-and-half mixture to melted chocolate; stir until smooth. Refrigerate until candy is firm but pliable. Beat with mixer until light and fluffy. Chill until firm enough to shape into balls. Form balls; dip into melted chocolate. Sprinkle with shaved chocolate while still soft.

Maple Creams

Makes 40 to 50 centers.

> 3 to 3½ cups dry fondant
> 2 tablespoons dry egg whites
> 6 tablespoons sweetened condensed milk
> 1 tablespoon light corn syrup
> 2 teaspoons maple flavoring
> ¼ teaspoon invertase
> ½ cup finely chopped walnuts
> 1 pound (approximately) real milk chocolate, melted for dipping

Combine ½ cup dry fondant and dry egg whites in bowl. Add condensed milk, corn syrup, flavoring and invertase; beat until light and smooth. Gradually add remaining dry fondant, first with mixer, then knead by hand; add nuts. Let set until fondant is dissolved. Form into balls. Dip in melted chocolate.

Easy Chocolate-Covered Creams

Makes approximately 120 centers.

> 2 pounds dry fondant
> ¾ cup butter, softened
> 3 tablespoons plus 1 teaspoon whipping cream
> Flavoring
> Food coloring
> Nuts
> Chopped dried *or* candied fruit
> 2½ pounds (approximately) real milk chocolate, melted for dipping

Combine fondant and butter; blend until mixture resembles coarse crumbs. Heat cream just to boiling point *(do not boil);* add to fondant mixture. Blend with spoon, then with hands until smooth and creamy. Add flavoring, food coloring, nuts and fruit as desired. Form into balls; dip in melted chocolate.

Butterscotch Creams

Makes approximately 50 centers.

- ¾ cup light brown sugar
- 1 cup granulated sugar
- ⅓ cup butter
- ¼ cup invert sugar
- ⅓ cup light corn syrup
- ⅓ cup frozen nondairy coffee creamer, thawed
- ⅛ teaspoon salt
- 4 drops butter flavoring
- 1 pound (approximately) real milk chocolate, melted for dipping

Combine all ingredients except butter flavoring and chocolate in large saucepan. Cook on high; then gradually lower heat as mixture thickens. Cook with minimum stirring to 240° on a candy thermometer. Pour onto marble slab; cool slightly. Fondant may need reheating as you work. (See introduction to fondant.) Work with spatula until candy becomes opaque and creamy. Spread soft mixture into buttered 9 x 13-inch pan. Let set several hours or overnight. Form into balls; dip in melted chocolate.

Tri-Flavor Easter Eggs

Makes 20 1-ounce eggs.

- 1 cup graham cracker crumbs
- 1 cup flaked coconut
- 3 cups confectioners' sugar
- 1 cup crunchy peanut butter
- ½ cup butter or margarine, melted
- 1 teaspoon vanilla
- ⅛ teaspoon salt
- ½ pound (approximately) butterscotch or chocolate-flavored compound coating, melted for dipping

Mix crumbs, coconut and 1½ cups confectioners' sugar together in bowl. Work in peanut butter, butter, vanilla and salt. Work in enough remaining confectioners' sugar by hand to shape centers easily. Shape into small eggs; dip in melted compound coating.

Easter Egg Candies

Makes approximately 60.

- 1 14.3-ounce box creamy white frosting mix
- 5 tablespoons butter, softened
- 3 tablespoons all-purpose flour
- 1 tablespoon light corn syrup
- 1½ tablespoons hot water
- 1¼ pounds (approximately) pastel-colored compound coating, melted for dipping

Combine frosting mix, butter and flour in bowl; set aside. Combine corn syrup and hot water; add to mixture in bowl. Blend with mixer until mixture resembles fine crumbs. Press into a ball with hands. Form into small egg shapes; dip in melted compound coating.

Note: For variety add desired amounts of melted real chocolate, candied fruit, nuts, coconut, flavorings or food colorings or use another frosting mix flavor.

Chocolate Easter Eggs

Makes 60 to 100.

- 1 pound confectioners' sugar
- 6 ounces semisweet chocolate-flavored compound coating, wafers or pieces, melted
- 1 3-ounce package cream cheese, softened
- 1 teaspoon vanilla
- 2½ to 3 tablespoons hot water
  Dash salt
- 2 pounds (approximately) real milk chocolate, melted for dipping
  Candy decorations, optional

Blend ½ pound confectioners' sugar, semisweet chocolate-flavored compound coating, cream cheese, vanilla, hot water and salt together with mixer. Work in remaining confectioners' sugar with hands. Form mixture into smooth, round ball; form small eggs. Dip in melted chocolate; decorate if desired.

Variation

Choco-Peanut Butter Easter Eggs: Divide mixture in half. To one half add 2 tablespoons peanut butter; form into small eggs. Repeat with remaining half or leave plain for basic Chocolate Easter Eggs. Dip in melted chocolate; decorate if desired.

Maple Nut Fudge

Makes approximately 80 pieces.

2¾ cups granulated sugar
¾ cup whole milk
¾ cup whipping cream
¾ cup invert sugar
¼ cup light corn syrup
¼ cup butter *or* margarine
¼ teaspoon salt
1 cup prepared Water Fondant, broken into pieces (Recipe on page 20)
1¾ cups plus 1 tablespoon marshmallow creme
1 teaspoon vanilla
1 teaspoon maple flavoring
1 cup finely chopped walnuts

Combine sugar, one-half each of the milk and cream, invert sugar, corn syrup, butter and salt in heavy 4-quart saucepan. Bring to rolling boil; stir occasionally. Add second half of milk and cream slowly; *do not* let candy stop boiling. Cook to 248° on a candy thermometer; stir occasionally. Remove from heat; cool candy to 205°. Add fondant and marshmallow creme; beat until well blended. Add flavorings and nuts; beat 2 more minutes. Spread candy into buttered 9-inch square pan. Cut into small squares.

Old-Fashioned White Fudge

Makes approximately 50 pieces.

2½ cups granulated sugar
¾ cup sour cream
¼ cup frozen nondairy coffee creamer, thawed
¼ teaspoon salt
2 teaspoons vanilla
¼ cup chopped candied cherries
1 cup coarsely chopped nuts

Combine sugar, sour cream, creamer and salt in heavy saucepan. Stir until sugar is moistened; cook to 238° on a candy thermometer without stirring. Immediately pour onto marble slab or cold surface; cool slightly. Work candy with fondant paddle; mix in vanilla. When fudge begins to lose its gloss, quickly add cherries and nuts; spread into buttered 8-inch square pan. Cut while still warm. Wrap individual pieces tightly in plastic wrap.

Rich Cream Fudge

Makes approximately 40 slices.

3 cups granulated sugar
1¼ cups whipping cream
1 cup light corn syrup
⅛ teaspoon salt
½ cup butter, softened
1 teaspoon vanilla
½ cup toasted sliced Brazil nuts *or* pecans

Combine sugar, cream, corn syrup and salt in heavy 3-quart saucepan; cook to 238° on a candy thermometer without stirring. Remove from heat; add butter and vanilla without stirring. Cool slightly. Beat with mixer until candy thickens and loses its gloss, approximately 40 minutes. Stir in nuts; quickly spread in buttered 9 x 5 x 3-inch loaf pan. Cool until firm. Remove from pan and wrap in foil or plastic wrap. Store in cool place. To serve, cut into thin slices.

Chocolate Fondant Fudge

Makes 64 pieces.

1½ cups granulated sugar
½ cup light corn syrup
1½ cups whipping cream
1 teaspoon salt
3 1-ounce squares baking chocolate, chopped
2 tablespoons butter, softened
1 cup prepared Water Fondant (Recipe on page 20)
2 teaspoons vanilla
½ cup coarsely chopped walnuts
1½ pounds (approximately) real milk chocolate, melted for dipping, optional

Combine sugar, corn syrup and ¾ cup cream in heavy saucepan. Bring to boil; add remaining cream slowly so boiling does not stop. Cook to 235° on a candy thermometer, lowering heat as mixture thickens. Remove from heat; add salt, chocolate and butter, without stirring. Cool slightly. Add fondant and vanilla; beat until candy thickens and loses its gloss. Blend in nuts. Spread in 9-inch square pan. Cut into pieces when cool; dip in melted chocolate, if desired.

Top: Old-Fashioned White Fudge (center), this page; Piña Colada Fudge, page 28.
Bottom, from Left: Maple Nut Fudge, this page; Creamy Butter Fudge, page 28; Black Walnut Fudge, page 29; Coconut Maple Creams, page 28; Chocolate Fondant Fudge, this page; Peanut Butter Fudge, page 28.

Fudge

Peanut Butter Fudge

Makes 64 1-inch squares.

- ½ pound real milk chocolate
- ½ pound white compound coating
- ½ pound peanut butter
- ¾ cup chopped blanched peanuts
- ¾ cup marshmallow creme
- ½ teaspoon salt

Melt real milk chocolate in double boiler over hot water. Melt compound coating in separate double boiler over hot water. Combine chocolate and compound coating; add remaining ingredients and beat until smooth. Spread in 8-inch square pan. Refrigerate until set; cut into squares.

Piña Colada Fudge

Makes approximately 80 pieces.

- 2 pounds yellow compound coating, wafers *or* pieces, melted
- 2 tablespoons paramount crystals, melted
- ¼ teaspoon butter rum concentrated flavoring
- ¼ teaspoon pineapple concentrated flavoring
- 1½ cups marshmallow creme
- 1½ cups pecans *or* other nuts
- ½ pound desiccated coconut
- 1 14-ounce can sweetened condensed milk

Combine all ingredients in large bowl; blend well. Spread mixture into foil-lined 9 x 13-inch pan. Let set overnight. Peel off foil and cut into pieces. Store in covered container.

Italian Delights

Makes 90 to 100 bars.

- 2¼ cups granulated sugar
- ⅔ cup light corn syrup
- 2 cups whipping cream
- 4 1-ounce squares baking chocolate, melted
- 1⅔ cups marshmallow creme
- ¾ cup prepared Water Fondant (Recipe on page 20)
- 1 teaspoon vanilla

Combine sugar, corn syrup and cream in heavy saucepan; cook to 244° on a candy thermometer, reducing heat as mixture thickens. Add chocolate; blend well. Add marshmallow creme and fondant; combine thoroughly. Add vanilla. Pour into buttered 9 x 13-inch pan. Let set; cut into small bars.

Coconut Maple Creams

Makes approximately 50.

- 2 cups granulated sugar
- ¼ cup invert sugar
- ½ cup milk
- ½ cup evaporated milk
- ½ teaspoon lecithin
- ⅛ teaspoon salt
- 1 cup maple syrup
- 2 tablespoons butter
- 20 large marshmallows, quartered
- 1½ cups flaked coconut

Combine sugars, milks, lecithin, salt and syrup in heavy saucepan; cook to 238° on a candy thermometer, stirring occasionally. Add butter and marshmallows; beat until fudge begins to get creamy. Add coconut; continue to beat a few minutes. Spread into buttered 8-inch square pan.

Note: Fudge may curdle, but will get smooth in beating process. A heavy-duty mixer may be used on medium speed. *Do not* use a hand mixer.

Creamy Butter Fudge

Makes approximately 50 pieces.

- 3 cups granulated sugar
- ½ cup cocoa
- ⅛ teaspoon salt
- 1 tablespoon unflavored gelatin
- 1 cup whipping cream
- ½ cup milk
- ¼ cup light corn syrup
- ½ cup butter
- ½ cup margarine
- 1½ teaspoons vanilla
- 1½ cups chopped walnuts *or* pecans

Combine all ingredients, except vanilla and nuts, in heavy 4-quart saucepan; blend well. Bring to rolling boil, stirring constantly. Continue to cook to 238° on a candy thermometer; gradually lower heat and stir gently. Remove from heat; pour into bowl. Cool 20 minutes; add vanilla and beat with mixer on low speed until creamy. Stir in nuts. Spread in 9-inch square pan. Cool and cut into squares.

Peanut Butter Squares

Makes 64.

- **2 cups granulated sugar**
- **⅔ cup evaporated milk**
- **1 cup peanut butter**
- **2 cups marshmallow creme**

Combine sugar and milk in heavy saucepan; cook to 238° on a candy thermometer, stirring constantly. Remove from heat; add peanut butter and marshmallow creme. Stir until smooth; spread into buttered 8-inch square pan. Cool and cut into squares.

Buttermilk Candy

Makes 64 pieces.

- **1 cup buttermilk**
- **1 teaspoon baking soda**
- **2 cups granulated sugar**
- **2 tablespoons light corn syrup**
- **¼ cup butter**
- **1 cup chopped pecans**

Combine buttermilk and baking soda in heavy saucepan; let stand 20 minutes. Add sugar and corn syrup; bring mixture to boil, stirring until sugar is dissolved. Add butter; cook to 238° on a candy thermometer, stirring occasionally. Candy will turn a medium brown. Cool slightly. Beat until candy loses its gloss and starts to thicken. Quickly stir in pecans; spread in buttered 8-inch square pan. Cut into squares.

Apple Fudge

Makes approximately 36 pieces.

- **3 cups granulated sugar**
- **¼ teaspoon salt**
- **2 tablespoons butter**
- **1 1-ounce square unsweetened chocolate, melted**
- **1½ cups peeled and grated apple with juice**
- **1 cup evaporated milk**
- **½ cup chopped nuts**
- **1 teaspoon vanilla**

Combine all ingredients, except nuts and vanilla, in heavy saucepan. Cook over medium heat; stir until sugar is dissolved. Continue to cook to 236° on a candy thermometer, stirring occasionally. Cool slightly. Beat until fudge is creamy and loses its gloss; add nuts and vanilla. Drop by spoonfuls onto waxed paper.

Black Walnut Fudge

Makes 64 1-inch pieces.

- **½ cup butter *or* margarine**
- **2¼ cups granulated sugar**
- **¾ cup frozen nondairy coffee creamer, thawed**
- **1 cup marshmallow creme**
- **⅛ teaspoon salt**
- **¾ pound (2⅓ cups) finely chopped real milk chocolate**
- **1 cup chopped black walnuts**
- **1 teaspoon vanilla**

Combine butter, sugar, creamer, marshmallow creme and salt in heavy 2½-quart saucepan. Bring to boil over medium heat; stir constantly until all ingredients are dissolved. Boil over medium heat 7 minutes; stir occasionally. Remove from heat; add chocolate, nuts and vanilla. Stir until chocolate is completely melted; beat 2 minutes. Pour into buttered 8-inch square pan. Cut into squares when cool.

Strawberry Jam Fudge

Makes approximately 50 pieces.

- **3 cups granulated sugar**
- **¼ teaspoon salt**
- **½ cup whipping cream**
- **⅓ cup water**
- **½ cup strawberry jam**
- **2 tablespoons butter**
- **1 tablespoon lemon juice**
- **Few drops red food coloring, optional**
- **½ pound real semisweet chocolate, melted**

Combine sugar, salt, cream and water in heavy saucepan; cook to 230° on a candy thermometer. Add jam, butter and lemon juice; continue to cook to 238°, stirring occasionally. Gradually lower heat as candy cooks; add food coloring, if desired. Pour onto cold surface or into shallow dish. Cool slightly; work candy with fondant paddle for approximately 20 minutes. If fudge is slow in creaming, rewarm on plate in microwave oven for a few seconds or on cookie sheet in warm oven; continue to work. When fudge begins to cream, spread into foil-lined 7-inch square pan. When firm, spread top of fudge with one-half of melted chocolate. When chocolate is firm, turn candy over on waxed paper; cover bottom with remaining melted chocolate. When firm, cut into small squares.

Chocolate Almond Toffee

Makes approximately 35 pieces.

    ½ cup butter, melted
    1½ cups light brown sugar
    2 tablespoons water
    1 tablespoon light corn syrup
    ½ package choco-bake or ½ 1-ounce square
       baking chocolate, melted
    ½ cup thinly sliced almonds, toasted and warm
    ¾ pound real semisweet chocolate, melted, optional

Combine butter, brown sugar, water and corn syrup in heavy saucepan; blend well. Cook to 230° on a candy thermometer; add chocolate and continue to cook to 294°. Pour into well-buttered 9 x 13-inch pan or onto buttered marble slab. Sprinkle almonds over top of hot toffee; press in with back of a spoon. Drizzle semisweet chocolate over toffee, if desired. Loosen from pan or slab before completely set. Cool and break into pieces.

Note: Almonds must be warm to adhere to candy.

Crunchy Nougat

Makes approximately 2 cups.

    1 cup granulated sugar
    3 drops lemon juice
    1 cup thinly sliced almonds, warmed
    ½ pound (approximately) real milk chocolate,
       melted for dipping, optional

Melt sugar in heavy skillet or saucepan; stir and watch carefully. Remove from heat before completely melted. Add lemon juice; blend well. Add almonds; stir until well coated. Spread as thin as possible onto buttered cookie sheet. Lift and stretch candy as it cools. Break into pieces and dip in chocolate, if desired. Store any uncoated nougat in air-tight container, as this candy picks up moisture and gets sticky if left exposed to air.

Variation

Crispy Nougat: Coarsely crush nougat; add equal amounts of crisp rice cereal and melted chocolate. Form into clusters; decorate each with a sliced almond.

Deluxe Brittle

Makes approximately 50 pieces.

    1 cup walnut pieces
    1 cup pecan pieces
    ½ cup whole pistachio nuts
    1 cup whole filberts
    1½ cups candied cherries
    1½ cups candied pineapple
    1 cup whole blanched toasted almonds
    2 cups granulated sugar
    1 cup water
    ¾ cup light corn syrup
    ½ teaspoon orange-flavored oil
       Orange food coloring

Combine all nuts except almonds and candied fruit in large bowl. Spread mixture ½ inch thick on well-oiled marble slab or cookie sheet; sprinkle with almonds. Combine sugar, water and corn syrup in heavy saucepan; cover with tight-fitting lid. When steam begins to escape, remove lid and insert candy thermometer. Cook to 300° without stirring. Remove from heat; add flavoring and coloring; stir only to blend. Drizzle syrup mixture over nut and fruit mixture in thin stream, back and forth, covering completely.* *Do not* scrape pan. When firm but not hard, cut into pieces. Store in covered container.

*Note: Do not mix fruit into syrup as it will change consistency of syrup. Always pour syrup over nuts and fruit. There may be some nuts and fruit that the syrup does not cover.

Sugared Almonds

Makes approximately 1 cup.

    1 cup granulated sugar
    ¼ cup water
    1 cup blanched almonds, dried thoroughly

Combine sugar and water in heavy saucepan; cook. Add almonds just before syrup spins a 2-inch thread when dropped from a spoon. Continue to cook, stirring to keep from scorching. When mixture begins to change color (caramelize), remove from heat. Stir until syrup crystalizes and clings to almonds. Spread almonds out individually on buttered cookie sheet to cool.

Tray, Clockwise from Left: Crispy Glazed Almonds, page 32; Almond Popcorn Crunch, page 32; Chocolate Almond Toffee, this page; Deluxe Brittle, this page.
Bottom, Clockwise from Left: Crunchy Nougat Dipped in Chocolate, this page; Peanut Butter Crunch, page 33; Brown Sugar Toffee, page 32; Rock Candy Suckers, page 33; Crunchy Nougat, this page.

Crunches

Butter Brickle

Makes approximately 40 pieces.

- 1¼ cups butter
- 2½ cups granulated sugar
- ½ cup water
- ½ teaspoon salt
- 1 cup pecans
- 1 pound (approximately) real milk chocolate, melted for dipping, optional

Combine butter and sugar in 2-quart saucepan; add water and salt. Heat and stir until sugar is dissolved. When mixture boils add nuts; cook to 290° on a candy thermometer, stirring constantly. Watch carefully as temperature increases so candy does not scorch. Pour onto buttered cookie sheet. Mark into squares as candy cools. Dip candy in melted chocolate, if desired, or wrap in plastic wrap.

Glazed Almonds

Makes approximately 1½ cups.

- 1 cup slivered almonds
- 2 tablespoons light corn syrup
- ¼ cup confectioners' sugar
- ½ cup real milk chocolate, melted for dipping

Combine almonds and corn syrup; add confectioners' sugar. Blend well; spread one layer thick onto buttered cookie sheet. Bake at 350° until golden. Loosen almonds from cookie sheet while still warm. When cool, break apart and dip in chocolate.

Variation

Crispy Glazed Almonds: Prepare Glazed Almonds as above; while warm break into small pieces. Add 1 cup crisp rice cereal or other crunchy cereal and melted chocolate; mix well. Drop onto buttered cookie sheet in clusters; let stand until cool.

Brown Sugar Toffee

Makes approximately 60 small pieces.

- 1 cup margarine
- 1½ cups dark brown sugar
- ½ teaspoon liquid lecithin
- ¾ cup pecans

Melt margarine in heavy 9- or 10-inch skillet. Add brown sugar; bring to boil, stirring con-stantly. When boiling, add lecithin. Continue to cook, stirring; gradually lower heat as mixture reaches 280° on a candy thermometer. Sprinkle pecans over buttered cookie sheet; pour mixture over pecans. When partially set, mark into squares with buttered knife. Cool and break into squares.

Sesame Seed Brittle

Makes approximately 30 small pieces.

- ⅓ cup butter
- 1 cup granulated sugar
- ⅛ teaspoon salt
- ½ teaspoon liquid lecithin
- ¾ cup sesame seed
- ½ pound (approximately) real milk chocolate, melted for dipping, optional

Melt butter in heavy 9- or 10-inch skillet; add sugar, salt and lecithin. Cook over medium heat, stirring occasionally, until sugar is melted and mixture is brown and bubbly. Add sesame seed; cook 1 minute, stirring gently. Pour into buttered 7 x 10-inch pan. While hot, mark into small squares with buttered knife. Dip in melted choco-late, if desired.

Almond Popcorn Crunch

Makes approximately 6 quarts.

- 2 cups granulated sugar
- 1 cup light brown sugar
- ¾ cup light corn syrup
- 1¼ cups water
- 1 tablespoon salt
- 1 cup whole *or* coarsely chopped almonds
- ½ cup butter, softened
- 6 quarts popped corn

Combine sugars, corn syrup, water and salt in 8-quart saucepan; cook to 235° on a candy thermometer. Add almonds; cook to 250°, stir-ring occasionally. Cook to 295°, stirring con-stantly. Add butter; stir until melted and com-pletely blended into syrup mixture. Remove from heat; add half the popped corn. Pour remaining popped corn into large buttered bowl. Stir syrup up from the bottom of pan, coating corn well. Pour this mixture over popped corn in bowl; stir until all corn is covered and almonds are distrib-uted evenly. Spread onto cold, buttered surface; break apart with two forks.

Butterscotch

Makes approximately 60 small pieces.

    2 cups granulated sugar
    ⅔ cup light corn syrup
    ¼ cup water
    2 tablespoons butter, softened
    1 teaspoon butter flavoring
      Yellow food coloring, optional

Combine sugar, corn syrup and water in heavy saucepan; cover with tight-fitting lid. Cook until steam escapes freely; remove lid, insert candy thermometer and cook to 250°. Add butter; cook to 290°. Remove from heat. Stir in butter flavoring; add food coloring, if desired. Pour onto well-buttered marble slab. Mark candy into squares with buttered knife; continue to mark as candy cools. When cool, break into pieces.

Super Caramel Corn

Makes approximately 8 cups.

    1 cup granola
    1 cup crisp rice cereal
    6 cups popped corn
    1 cup butter
    1 cup granulated sugar
    2 tablespoons water
    1 tablespoon light corn syrup
    1 teaspoon salt

Combine cereals and popped corn in large buttered bowl; set aside. Melt butter in 3-quart saucepan. Add sugar, water, corn syrup and salt; cook to 272° on a candy thermometer, stirring occasionally. Lower heat as mixture thickens. Remove from heat; pour over cereal and popcorn mixture, stirring to coat well. Spread onto buttered cookie sheet; break into pieces when cool.

Peanut Butter Crunch

Makes approximately 40 small pieces.

    1 cup peanut butter
    1 tablespoon butter
    ½ teaspoon vanilla
    ⅛ teaspoon salt
    1 cup granulated sugar
    ⅓ cup light corn syrup
    ⅓ cup water
    1 pound (approximately) real milk chocolate, melted for dipping, optional

Heat peanut butter, butter, vanilla and salt in double boiler over hot water. Combine sugar, corn syrup and water in separate saucepan; cook to 305° on a candy thermometer. Remove from heat. Quickly add warm peanut butter mixture; stir until completely blended. Immediately pour into 11 x 15-inch buttered pan. Spread as thin as possible. Mark into pieces immediately. When cool, break into pieces. Dip in melted chocolate, if desired.

Almond Brittle

Makes approximately 35 pieces.

    1 cup coarsely chopped almonds
    1 cup butter*
    1⅓ cups granulated sugar
    1 tablespoon light corn syrup
    3 tablespoons water
    ¾ pound (approximately) real milk chocolate, melted, optional
    ¾ cup finely chopped nuts, optional

Spread almonds in shallow pan; toast at 250 — 300° until nuts are lightly browned. Leave in oven at 200° until ready to use. Melt butter in heavy 2-quart saucepan; add sugar, corn syrup and water. Cook to 300° on a candy thermometer, stirring only as necessary with thermometer; lower heat as candy thickens. Quickly stir in warm nuts. Spread onto buttered marble slab or cookie sheet; cool completely. Turn onto waxed paper; spread with melted chocolate and sprinkle with nuts, if desired. Break into pieces when cool.

*Note: Do not use a substitute for butter.

Rock Candy Suckers

Makes 12.

    1 cup granulated sugar
    ⅓ cup light corn syrup
    ½ cup water
      Flavoring oil
      Food coloring

Combine sugar, corn syrup and water in small saucepan; cover with tight-fitting lid. When steam escapes from under lid, remove lid and insert candy thermometer. Cook to 300°, without stirring. Add flavoring and coloring; blend well. Pour into prepared sucker forms or in mounds on well-buttered cookie sheets. Let stand to harden.

Miscellaneous

Carmelo Swirl and Choco-Carmelo Swirl Candy

Makes approximately 48 pieces.

> ½ recipe Fluffy Marshmallow Candy (Recipe on page 40)
> 1 pound caramel, purchased *or* homemade
> 2 cups dry-roasted peanuts
> 1¼ cups finely chopped real semisweet chocolate

Fold a 24-inch strip of foil lengthwise to make a 2 x 24-inch strip. Fold each end in to make a strip 17 inches long. Butter strip on both sides and stand on its side in the center of a buttered 9 x 13-inch pan, making two sections, each 9 x 6½-inches; set aside. Prepare marshmallow as directed in recipe. While beating marshmallow, melt caramel in microwave or in saucepan over low heat. Pour half of beaten marshmallow in one-half of prepared pan. Add peanuts to caramel; blend well. Spread half of caramel-peanut mixture over marshmallow; quickly marble mixture with a knife. Blend 1 cup semisweet chocolate into remaining half of marshmallow in mixer. Beat until chocolate is melted into marshmallow; pour into other half of prepared pan. Add ¼ cup semisweet chocolate to remaining caramel-nut mixture; stir until melted and blended. Pour mixture in thin stream over chocolate-marshmallow mixture. Marble, if desired. Let candies stand overnight. Cut into squares with a scissors; wrap in plastic wrap.

Twisted Kentucky Creams

Makes approximately 60.

> 2 cups granulated sugar
> ½ cup water
> ¼ teaspoon salt
> ⅛ teaspoon baking soda
> ½ cup whipping cream

Butter marble slab or three cookie sheets; chill. Combine sugar, water, salt and baking soda in saucepan; cover with tight-fitting lid and cook for a few minutes over medium heat. Remove lid, insert candy thermometer and cook to 250°. Add cream slowly so boiling does not stop. Cook again to 250°. Pour in thin strips on marble slab or chilled cookie sheets; let stand 5 minutes. Pick up ribbons, one at a time, and pull until they are ivory in color and stiff. Twist into a rope; cut into 1½-inch pieces. Place on buttered cookie sheets. Cover with waxed paper; let stand 3 to 4 hours. Candy will change from chewy to creamy. Store in airtight container.

Rocky Road Candy

Makes approximately 2 pounds.

> 1½ pounds real milk chocolate *or* milk chocolate-flavored compound coating, wafers *or* pieces
> Paramount crystals *or* corn oil (approximately 2 tablespoons per pound)
> ¼ recipe Fluffy Marshmallow Candy (Recipe on page 40) *or* 1 small bag, purchased, cut up
> 1½ cups coarsely chopped roasted almonds *or* pecans

Melt chocolate and crystals together in double boiler over hot water (if real milk chocolate is used, temper it—see introduction). Cool chocolate to about 84°; at this point either add marshmallows and nuts and spread mixture in buttered 2-inch deep pan *or* line bottom and sides of pan with half of melted chocolate, sprinkle marshmallows and nuts on chocolate and pour remaining melted chocolate over marshmallows and nuts to completely seal. *Do not* cut until ready to serve.

Pecan Chews

Makes 20.

> ½ pound soft caramel, purchased *or* homemade
> 2 tablespoons heavy cream
> 1¼ cups pecan halves
> Real milk chocolate, melted for dipping

Heat caramel and heavy cream in double boiler over hot, not boiling, water until caramel is melted. Place nuts in 20 paper candy cups. Cool caramel mixture a few minutes; drop spoonfuls of caramel over nuts. Let stand until firm. Cover caramel with melted chocolate.

From Top: Carmelo Swirls, this page; Chocolate Marshmallows, page 40; Nougat Loaf, page 37; Sno-Caps, page 40; Deluxe Commercial Nougat, page 37; Pecan Chews in Paper Cups, this page; Choco-Carmelo Swirls, this page.

Miscellaneous

Pistachio Nougat

Makes approximately 2½ pounds.

Part I

- ¾ cup granulated sugar
- ⅔ cup light corn syrup
- ¼ cup water
- 1 large egg white

Combine sugar, corn syrup and water in small saucepan; blend well. Cover with tight-fitting lid and cook until steam escapes freely from under lid. Remove lid, insert candy thermometer and cook without stirring to 238°. Beat egg white until stiff peaks form. Pour cooked syrup mixture slowly over beaten egg white, beating constantly. Beat until mixture is thick and lukewarm, 8 to 10 minutes; set aside.

Part II

- 1½ cups granulated sugar
- 1½ cups light corn syrup
- ¼ cup butter, room temperature
- 2 teaspoons vanilla
  Green food coloring, optional
- ½ teaspoon salt
- 1 cup chopped pistachios
- 1¾ pounds (approximately) real milk chocolate, melted for dipping, optional

Combine sugar and corn syrup in saucepan; blend well. Insert candy thermometer; cook to 272°. Pour hot syrup over Part I mixture; beat until well blended. Add butter, vanilla and food coloring, if desired; blend thoroughly. Stir in salt and nuts; pour into well-buttered 9 x 13-inch pan. Let set several hours or overnight. Cut and wrap in plastic wrap or dip in melted chocolate, if desired.

Marshmallow Creme or Frappé

Makes approximately 3½ quarts.

- 2¼ cups invert sugar
- 4½ tablespoons dried egg whites
- 2¼ cups light corn syrup
- 1 teaspoon vanilla

Combine 1⅛ cups invert sugar with egg whites in bowl; blend with mixer on low speed. Combine remaining invert sugar and corn syrup in saucepan; heat to 210° on a candy thermometer. Slowly add syrup to egg white mixture, beating constantly. Add vanilla; continue to beat until mixture doubles in volume and becomes white and fluffy. Store in covered container.

Note: This mixture does not need to be refrigerated. It keeps well indefinitely in covered container. If mixture should separate, blend well before using.

Gelatin Gumdrops

Makes 80 to 90.

- Vegetable oil spray
- 3 6-ounce packages flavored gelatin
- 1 teaspoon unflavored gelatin
- 2 cups cold water
  Pinch salt
  Granulated sugar

Spray small molds with vegetable oil spray. Combine gelatins in saucepan; add water and salt. Boil 1 minute; pour into molds. Refrigerate until firm. Remove from molds and roll in granulated sugar.

Soft Maple Nougat

Makes approximately 40 pieces.

- 3 cups light brown sugar
- 2 tablespoons light corn syrup
- 1 cup boiling water
- ⅛ teaspoon salt
- 3 medium egg whites
- 2 teaspoons vanilla
- 1 teaspoon maple flavoring
- 1 cup finely chopped nuts

Combine brown sugar, corn syrup, water and salt in 2-quart saucepan; cover and cook a few minutes. Remove lid; insert candy thermometer and cook to 250°*. *Do not stir.* Beat egg whites in separate bowl until stiff peaks form; pour hot syrup mixture into egg whites. Add flavorings and continue to beat until creamy. Blend in nuts. Pour into buttered foil-lined 4½ x 8½ x 2½-inch loaf pan. Let stand several hours. Slice and fit into chocolate-lined candy bar molds.

Note: For firmer nougat cook to 265°.

Nougat Loaf

Makes approximately 30 pieces.

- 2 tablespoons confectioners' sugar
- 2 cups granulated sugar
- ½ cup light corn syrup
- ½ cup hot water
- ⅛ teaspoon salt
- 2 tablespoons butter
- ⅓ cup frozen nondairy coffee creamer, thawed
- 1 tablespoon marshmallow creme
- 1 cup slivered almonds, toasted
- 1 teaspoon vanilla
- ¾ pound (approximately) real milk chocolate, melted for dipping, optional

Butter a 7½ x 3⅞ x 2¼-inch loaf pan. Generously sprinkle confectioners' sugar over buttered surface. Combine granulated sugar, corn syrup, water and salt in 2-quart saucepan; cook to 270° on a candy thermometer. Remove from heat; add butter and creamer. Return to heat; watch closely and cook to 238°, lowering heat as mixture thickens. Remove from heat. Pour cooked syrup mixture into bowl of heavy-duty mixer or let cool in saucepan to about 230°. Beat until creamy; add marshmallow creme, nuts and vanilla. Pour into prepared loaf pan. Sprinkle confectioners' sugar over top of candy. Let stand 24 hours in cool place. Cut into slices and cut each slice in half. Wrap in plastic wrap or dip in chocolate, if desired.

Deluxe Commerical Nougat

Makes approximately 100 pieces.

- 3 tablespoons dry egg whites
- 2 tablespoons water
- ¼ cup invert sugar
- 2 cups granulated sugar
- ⅓ cup water
- ⅔ cup invert sugar
- 1 cup light corn syrup
  Dash salt
- 2 tablespoons vegetable shortening
- 1 teaspoon vanilla
- 1 cup roasted, slivered almonds
- 2 pounds (approximately) real milk chocolate, melted for dipping, optional

Blend egg whites with 2 tablespoons water in bowl; beat until soft peaks form. Gradually add ¼ cup invert sugar; continue to beat until mixture is light and fluffy. Set aside. Combine granulated sugar, ⅓ cup water, ⅔ cup invert sugar, corn syrup and salt in heavy saucepan; cook to 250° on a candy thermometer. Pour half of cooked syrup mixture over beaten egg whites. Cook remaining syrup to 285°; add to egg white mixture and continue to beat until soft peaks form. Blend in shortening, vanilla and nuts. Pour into buttered 9 x 13-inch pan. Let stand overnight. Cut and wrap in plastic wrap or dip in melted chocolate, if desired.

Homemade Sweetened Condensed Milk

Makes approximately 1 cup.

- 1 cup instant dry nonfat milk
- ⅔ cup granulated sugar
- ⅓ cup boiling water
- ¼ cup butter, melted

Combine all ingredients in blender; blend until smooth, scraping down sides occasionally.

Chocolate Malted Milk Nougat

Makes approximately 40 pieces.

- 1 cup granulated sugar
- ⅓ cup light corn syrup
- ⅓ cup water
- 1 egg white
- ½ 1-ounce square baking chocolate, finely chopped
- 3 tablespoons malted milk powder
  Pinch salt
- ½ pound (approximately) real milk chocolate, melted for dipping, optional

Combine sugar, corn syrup and water in heavy saucepan; cook to 260° on a candy thermometer. Beat egg white; pour cooked syrup mixture over egg white. Continue to beat constantly until stiff peaks form. Add baking chocolate, malted milk powder and salt; beat until creamy. Spread in buttered 8-inch square pan. When cool, cut and wrap or dip in melted chocolate.

Miscellaneous

Walnut Slices

Makes 3 6-inch rolls.

- ½ cup whipping cream
- ½ cup whole milk
- 1 cup light brown sugar
- 2 cups granulated sugar
- ¼ cup light corn syrup
- ⅛ teaspoon salt
- ⅓ cup miniature marshmallows
- 1 teaspoon vanilla
- 1 teaspoon black walnut flavoring
- 1½ cups finely chopped walnuts

Combine cream, milk, sugars, corn syrup and salt in heavy 3-quart saucepan. Cook to 238° on a candy thermometer, stirring occasionally. Add marshmallows; pour onto marble slab. Cool to comfortably warm; then work with fondant paddle or spoon. Add vanilla and walnut flavoring while working. When mixture starts to set add ½ cup walnuts. Continue to work candy until it creams. Form into 3 rolls; press one-third remaining nuts into each roll. Wrap rolls in plastic wrap. Slice to serve.

Popcorn Patties

Makes approximately 24.

- 1¼ cups coarsely chopped popped corn
- ½ cup coarsely chopped roasted peanuts
- ½ cup light brown sugar
- ¼ cup granulated sugar
- ¼ cup light corn syrup
- ½ cup water
- ¼ teaspoon salt
- 1 tablespoon molasses
- 1 tablespoon butter
- ⅛ teaspoon baking soda

Place popcorn and nuts in oven at 250° to warm. Combine sugars, corn syrup, water and salt in heavy saucepan; cook covered until steam escapes freely from under lid. Remove lid; insert candy thermometer and cook to 270°, watching closely after 260°. Add molasses and butter at 270°; cook to 275°, stirring constantly with thermometer or spoon. Remove from heat; add baking soda and stir until dissolved. Quickly add warm popcorn and nuts; blend well. Quickly spoon small amounts of candy into buttered muffin cups; pat each with fork to flatten. Cool.

Invert Sugar

Makes approximately 8 pounds.

- 8 pounds granulated sugar
- 1 quart water
- ½ ounce citric acid or the juice of 4 lemons

Combine all ingredients in heavy 8-quart kettle. Bring to a boil, stirring constantly so mixture does not scorch. Lower heat and simmer for ½ hour, stirring constantly.

Pecan Rolls

Makes 20.

- 2½ cups granulated sugar
- ½ cup light corn syrup
- ½ cup water
- 2 cups marshmallow creme
- 1 teaspoon vanilla
- ⅓ cup vegetable shortening
- ¼ cup chopped nuts or candied fruit, optional
- 1 cup confectioners' sugar
- 2 pounds chopped pecans

Combine granulated sugar, corn syrup and water in heavy saucepan; cover and cook until steam escapes freely from under lid. Remove lid; insert candy thermometer. Cook to 256°, without stirring. Remove from heat; add marshmallow creme without stirring. Let stand 10 minutes. Beat until mixture "breaks short";* add vanilla while beating. Add shortening; blend well. Add nuts or fruit, if desired. Sprinkle confectioners' sugar on slab; pour mixture onto sugar and form into rolls. Dip rolls into Caramel Coating, then roll in chopped pecans to completely cover.

Caramel Coating

- 1½ cups granulated sugar
- 1 cup light corn syrup
- 1 cup sweetened condensed milk
- ¾ cup vegetable shortening
- 1½ cups whipping cream

Combine all ingredients in heavy saucepan; cook to 242° on a candy thermometer, stirring constantly.

*Note: Mixture "breaks short" when beaters are lifted and candy snaps off.

Clockwise, from Top Left: Pecan Rolls, this page; Popcorn Patties, this page; Puffed Wheat TV Snacks, page 41; Walnut Slices, this page; Quick Pralines, page 41; Sliced Pecan Roll.

Miscellaneous

Fluffy Marshmallow Candy

Makes approximately 100 pieces.

- ¼ cup unflavored gelatin
- ½ cup cold water
- ½ cup warm water
- 2½ cups granulated sugar
- 1½ cups invert sugar
- ¾ cup light corn syrup
- 1 teaspoon vanilla
- 2 cups toasted coconut *or* confectioners' sugar, *or* 2 pounds (approximately) real milk chocolate, melted for dipping, optional

Soak gelatin in cold water in bowl. Combine warm water and sugars in saucepan; cook to 210° on a candy thermometer. Pour hot mixture over softened gelatin and beat. Add corn syrup and vanilla; continue to beat until mixture is white and doubled in volume. Pour into buttered 12 x 15-inch pan; let stand 24 hours before cutting into squares.* If desired roll squares in toasted coconut *or* confectioners' sugar *or* dip in melted chocolate.

*Note: To cut marshmallows before standing 24 hours—heat corn syrup with sugar mixture, instead of adding later.

Caramel-Mallow Roll-Ups

Makes approximately 48.

- ½ pound caramel, purchased *or* homemade, cut into small pieces
- ½ recipe Fluffy Marshmallow Candy (Recipe on page 40)
- 1 pound (approximately) real milk chocolate, melted for dipping, optional

Place caramel in buttered 8-inch square pan. Bake at 200° a few minutes until caramel melts and flows evenly over bottom of pan; let cool. Prepare marshmallow as directed in recipe; spread over caramel, equal in depth to caramel. Chill until caramel firms. Cut into 3 sections and roll each section into a log. Wrap in plastic wrap; refrigerate. Slice roll into ½-inch pieces; wrap each slice in plastic wrap or dip each slice in melted chocolate. Spread leftover marshmallow in a buttered pan and follow directions for Fluffy Marshmallow Candy.

Note: Leftover marshmallow will keep several weeks.

Mint Marshmallows

Makes 25 to 30.

- ¼ recipe Fluffy Marshmallow Candy (Recipe on page 40)
- 2 to 4 drops peppermint oil
  Green food coloring
- ½ pound (approximately) real sweet or semisweet chocolate, melted for dipping

Prepare marshmallow as directed in recipe, but when almost doubled in volume add peppermint oil and food coloring. Spread in buttered 9-inch square pan. When set, cut into squares; dip in melted chocolate.

Sno-Caps

Makes approximately 30.

- 2 cups granulated sugar
- ½ cup water
- ¼ teaspoon cream of tartar
  Pinch salt
- 2 cups marshmallow creme
- ½ cup nuts
- 1 teaspoon vanilla
- ¾ pound (approximately) real semisweet chocolate, melted for dipping

Combine sugar, water, cream of tartar and salt in saucepan; cook, covered with tight-fitting lid. When steam escapes freely from under lid, remove lid and insert candy thermometer; cook to 250°. Pour cooked syrup over marshmallow creme in bowl; beat until soft peaks form and mixture becomes creamy. *Do not underbeat.* Add nuts and vanilla; blend well. Drop by teaspoonfuls onto waxed paper. When set, dip bottoms of candy into melted semisweet chocolate; place on waxed paper until chocolate is set.

Note: To dip—put fork well below surface of melted chocolate in double boiler over hot water. Drop set candy into chocolate, right side up. Bring fork up under candy and lift out, tapping on side of pan to remove excess chocolate.

Quick Pralines

Makes approximately 20.

¼ cup butter
½ cup light brown sugar
¼ cup whipping cream
1 cup dry fondant
1½ cups pecan pieces
20 whole pecans, optional

Melt butter in heavy 1-quart saucepan; add brown sugar and bring to boil. Boil 1 minute, stirring constantly. Remove from heat; stir in cream. Return to heat and bring to boil, stirring constantly. When boiling, remove from heat; stir in dry fondant and blend until smooth. Stir in pecan pieces; drop by teaspoonfuls onto waxed paper. Garnish with whole pecans, if desired.

Note: A heavy saucepan is important as butter and sugar will scorch easily.

Chocolate-Covered Cherries

Makes 48.

3 tablespoons butter *or* margarine,
   room temperature
¾ cup marshmallow creme
1 tablespoon invert sugar
½ teaspoon almond flavoring
¼ teaspoon vanilla
   Pinch salt
3 drops invertase
2½ cups sifted confectioners' sugar
1 pound real semisweet chocolate, for dipping
48 small maraschino cherries, drained

Combine butter and marshmallow creme in bowl. Add invert sugar, flavorings, salt, invertase and half of confectioners' sugar; beat well. Gradually add remaining confectioners' sugar, a little at a time, kneading in by hand; add more if necessary to form firm dough that is not sticky. Melt semisweet chocolate in double boiler over hot water.* Take small pieces of candy mixture and wrap each cherry; dip each in melted chocolate, using a fork or dipping fork. Fondant will turn to liquid in about 5 days.

*Note: If using real chocolate, temper (see introduction). If using compound coating, cool slightly before dipping.

Half-Baked Candy

Makes approximately 80 pieces.

1 egg white
1 cup light brown sugar
1 cup ground pecans *or* walnuts
1 cup granulated sugar
⅛ teaspoon salt
½ cup milk
½ cup whipping cream
1 tablespoon light corn syrup
2 tablespoons cocoa
2 tablespoons butter

Place egg white in bowl; beat until soft peaks form. Gradually add brown sugar while beating. Fold in ground nuts; spread nut mixture evenly in buttered 9 x 13-inch pan. Bake at 300° 10 to 15 minutes or until lightly browned. (Watch carefully so it does not burn.) Set aside to cool. Combine remaining ingredients in 2-quart saucepan; cook to 238° on a candy thermometer, stirring with thermometer only as necessary. Cool slightly in saucepan or on marble slab. Beat candy until it begins to hold shape; spread quickly over cooled nut mixture. Cut into squares immediately.

Puffed Wheat TV Snacks

Makes 40 2-inch-square pieces.

9 cups puffed wheat
1 cup salted peanuts
2 cups granulated sugar
1 cup hot water
¼ cup light corn syrup
2 teaspoons vinegar
1 teaspoon salt
3 tablespoons butter
½ teaspoon baking soda

Place puffed wheat and peanuts on cookie sheet; warm in oven at 200°. Combine sugar, water, corn syrup, vinegar and salt in 2-quart saucepan; cover tightly and cook until steam escapes freely from under lid. Remove lid; insert candy thermometer. Cook to 280° without stirring. Remove from heat; add butter and baking soda. Stir to dissolve; blend well. Place cereal and nuts in buttered 12-quart bowl or kettle; pour syrup mixture over and stir until well coated. Spread candy onto buttered cookie sheet. Cut into squares when set.

Easy Fondant for Dipping Fruit

Makes approximately 80.

    4 cups dry fondant
    3 drops butter flavoring
    1 tablespoon light corn syrup
    ¼ cup water
    ½ teaspoon vanilla
      Food coloring and flavoring, if desired
      Fruit (strawberries, cherries, orange sections,
      pineapple chunks)
    1 pound (approximately) real milk chocolate,
      melted for dipping, optional

Combine dry fondant, butter flavoring, corn syrup, water and vanilla in double boiler over hot water. Stir until blended and mixture is smooth and fluid. Add food coloring and flavoring, if desired. Dip fruit into fondant, holding by stem or with fingertips or toothpick. Let dry on waxed paper. Fruit may then be dipped, partially or totally, in melted chocolate, if desired.

Note: Fruit does not keep well and should be served within a few hours.

Buttermilk Pralines

Makes approximately 25.

    2 cups granulated sugar
    1 teaspoon baking soda
    ¼ cup dry buttermilk powder
    ⅛ teaspoon salt
    1 cup water
    2 tablespoons butter
    2 cups pecans
    1 teaspoon vanilla
      Whole pecans for garnish, optional

Combine sugar, baking soda, buttermilk powder and salt in 4-quart saucepan; add water and butter. Cook over medium heat to 215° on a candy thermometer, stirring gently. Add 2 cups pecans and continue to cook, stirring constantly, to 230°. Remove from heat; cool 10 minutes in saucepan. Add vanilla; beat until mixture begins to thicken. Quickly drop by teaspoonfuls onto buttered foil. Garnish each with whole pecans, if desired. These are slightly sugary, typical of traditional pralines.

Cream Cheese Fondant for Cherries

Makes 48 to 50.

    1 3-ounce package cream cheese, room
      temperature
    3 tablespoons butter, room temperature
      Pinch salt
    ¼ teaspoon almond flavoring
    ¼ teaspoon vanilla
    2½ to 3 cups confectioners' sugar
    48 to 50 maraschino cherries
    1 pound (approximately) sweet *or* semisweet
      chocolate-flavored compound coating, melted for
      dipping

Combine cream cheese, butter, salt and flavorings in bowl; blend well. Add confectioners' sugar, a little at a time, first with a spoon, then knead with your hands until candy loses its stickiness and forms a smooth ball. Divide into 3 parts; form each into 1¼-inch diameter log. Slice each log into ⅛-inch slices. Flatten each slice, place maraschino cherry in center and form fondant around cherry. Shape in palms of hands to form smooth ball. Dip in melted compound coating. Check cherries in a few hours to see if there are any leaks; patch leaks with a brush dipped in melted compound coating.

Spiced Nuts

Makes approximately 2 cups.

    1 egg white, lightly beaten
    1½ tablespoons cold water
    1 cup confectioners' sugar
    2 tablespoons cornstarch
    1 teaspoon salt
    ¼ teaspoon cinnamon
    ¼ teaspoon cloves
    ¼ teaspoon allspice
    1 cup walnut halves
    1 cup pecan halves

Blend egg white and water in small bowl. Combine remaining ingredients except nuts in separate bowl. Dip nuts, a few at a time, first in egg white mixture, then in dry ingredients, removing nuts with a fork. Place nuts, flat side down, on greased cookie sheet. Bake at 250° 1 hour. Sift excess coating from nuts gently; store in covered container.

Note: Substitute 2 cups blanched almonds for walnut and pecan halves; bake at 250° 3 hours.

Tin, Top Left: Creamy Fudge (with nuts), page 44;
Five-Minute Fudge, page 44.
Tin, Top Right: Pecan Brittle, page 45; Peanut Brittle, page 44.
Plate: Choco-Mallo Treats (center), page 45;
Crunchy Cups, page 45.

Candy and Candy Molding Cookbook 43

Microwave

Creamy Fudge

Makes 50 to 60 pieces.

  3 cups granulated sugar
½ cup butter
¼ teaspoon salt
⅔ cup frozen nondairy coffee creamer, thawed
  2 cups semisweet chocolate-flavored compound coating, wafers *or* pieces
  2 cups marshmallow creme
  1 teaspoon vanilla
  1 cup chopped pecans *or* walnuts
50 or 60 pecans *or* walnut halves, optional

Combine sugar, butter, salt and creamer in buttered 3-quart baking dish; cook on full power 6 minutes or until mixture comes to a full rolling boil, stirring once or twice. Cook additional 3 minutes. Remove from microwave; add compound coating and stir until melted. Add marshmallow creme, vanilla and chopped nuts; beat 5 minutes or until a spoonful dropped back in bowl maintains its shape a few seconds. Pour into buttered 9 x 13-inch pan. Mark pieces; place a pecan on each piece, if desired. Cover with plastic wrap and refrigerate 3 to 5 hours. Cut into squares.

Note: Real chocolate may be substituted for compound coating.

Five-Minute Fudge

Makes approximately 36 pieces.

  1 pound confectioners' sugar, sifted
⅓ cup cocoa, sifted
¼ cup frozen nondairy coffee creamer, thawed
¼ pound butter *or* margarine, cut into pieces
    Few grains salt
  1 teaspoon vanilla
½ cup chopped pecans *or* walnuts

Combine confectioners' sugar and cocoa in 2-quart glass baking dish. Add creamer and butter; blend well. (Mixture will look dry.) Cook in microwave on full power 2 minutes. Remove from oven; beat until all ingredients are well blended. Add salt, vanilla and nuts; pour into buttered 8-inch square pan. Chill 1 to 2 hours; cut into squares.

Microwave Peanut Butter Fudge

Makes approximately 36 pieces.

  1 pound real milk chocolate
  1 cup peanut butter

Place chocolate in glass bowl. Microwave on full power 1 minute; stir and cook an additional 30 seconds. Stir until completely melted. Add peanut butter; blend well. Pour into foil-lined 7-inch square pan. When cool cut into squares.

Note: Substitute butterscotch, peanut butter or white compound coating for real milk chocolate for variations in flavor.

Peanut Clusters

Makes approximately 90.

  1 pound white compound coating, wafers *or* pieces
  1 cup semisweet chocolate-flavored compound coating, wafers *or* pieces
  1 cup sweet chocolate-flavored compound coating, wafers *or* pieces
  2 cups roasted peanuts

Place compound coatings in glass bowl; microwave on high power 1 minute. Remove from oven and stir. Microwave 1 minute; remove and stir. Repeat if necessary but remove before compound coatings are completely melted; stir to complete melting. When well blended, stir in peanuts; drop onto waxed paper in clusters.

Peanut Brittle

Makes approximately 1 pound.

  1 cup granulated sugar
½ cup water
½ teaspoon salt
½ cup light corn syrup
¾ cup chopped raw peanuts
½ teaspoon vanilla
  1 teaspoon baking soda
  1 tablespoon butter

Butter a 2-quart glass baking dish. Combine sugar, water, salt and corn syrup in dish; cook in microwave oven on full power 15 minutes, stirring twice. Cook to 240° on a microwave candy thermometer; stir in nuts. Watch closely; continue to cook to 300°. Syrup mixture will be light golden brown. Remove from oven; stir in vanilla, baking soda and butter. Blend thoroughly; pour as thin as possible onto a well-buttered marble slab or cookie sheet. Let stand a few minutes. While still hot flip candy over and pull it as thin as possible, being careful not to burn your fingers.

Crunchy Cups

Makes approximately 50.

      1 pound white compound coating, wafers or pieces
      1 cup crisp rice cereal
      1 cup miniature marshmallows
   ½ cup broken pretzel pieces
      1 cup natural or granola cereal
      1 cup roasted peanuts
   50 candied cherry halves
   50 pieces candied pineapple

Place compound coating in glass bowl; microwave on full power 1 minute. Stir and microwave 1 minute. Remove; stir to finish melting and blend in remaining ingredients except candied fruit. Spoon mixture into paper candy cups; garnish with pieces of candied cherries and pineapple.

Butterscotch Fudge

Makes approximately 50 pieces.

   ½ cup butter
      1 cup granulated sugar
   ⅓ cup light brown sugar
   ⅔ cup frozen nondairy coffee creamer, thawed
   ⅛ teaspoon salt
   2½ cups butterscotch compound coating, wafers or pieces
      2 cups miniature marshmallows
   ½ teaspoon vanilla
      1 pound (approximately) real milk chocolate, melted for dipping, optional

Combine butter, sugars, creamer and salt in 2-quart glass baking dish. Cook in microwave to 238° on a microwave candy thermometer; stir every 4 minutes and check thermometer. Remove from oven; add compound coating, marshmallows and vanilla. Beat until well blended. Spread in buttered 9-inch square pan. When cool cut into squares or roll into a log shape and slice. Dip into melted chocolate, if desired.

Pecan Brittle

Makes approximately 30 pieces.

      5 cups pecans
      2 cups granulated sugar
   ⅓ cup light corn syrup
      1 cup butter
   ½ teaspoon salt
      1 teaspoon baking soda
      1 teaspoon vanilla

Toast pecans on cookie sheet at 200° in a conventional oven 30 minutes; leave in oven to keep warm until ready to use. Combine sugar and corn syrup in 3-quart glass baking dish; microwave on full power 2 minutes. Stir and turn bowl. Microwave 2 minutes; stir and turn. Microwave 5 minutes; candy should be turning caramel color. Watch closely; continue to microwave to 310° on a microwave candy thermometer or until light golden brown in color. *Do not* let mixture scorch. Remove from microwave; add butter and return to oven. Microwave until butter is completely melted and mixture is at a rolling boil, about 290°. Remove from oven. Stir in salt, baking soda and vanilla. Stir quickly to blend; add warm pecans. Spread onto well-buttered marble slab or cookie sheet. As candy cools loosen from bottom and flip; pull candy to make as thin as possible.

Coco-Mallo Treats

Makes approximately 48.

      2 eggs
   1½ cups confectioners' sugar
      1 teaspoon vanilla
   ⅛ teaspoon salt
      2 cups semisweet chocolate-flavored compound coating, wafers or pieces
      2 tablespoons butter
      2 cups dry-roasted peanuts
      2 cups miniature marshmallows

Beat eggs until fluffy; add sugar, vanilla and salt. Blend well. Place chocolate-flavored compound coating and butter in 2-quart glass baking dish. Microwave on full power 1 minute. Stir and microwave 30 seconds. Remove; stir until completely melted and smooth. Add to egg mixture. Beat well; stir in nuts and marshmallows. Drop into candy cups or onto waxed paper in clusters. Chill. Store in refrigerator.

Candy Molding Basics

Molding Chocolate

With the use of chocolate-flavored coatings, chocolate molding has become easy, and excellent results can be realized with minimum effort. An endless number of molds are available: chicks and rabbits for Easter, Santas and suckers for Christmas, witches for Halloween, and molds for every occasion.

Chocolate-flavored coatings are easiest to mold. To prepare coatings, melt in double boiler over hot (never boiling) water, or place in a wide-mouth glass jar and set in a hot water bath. Stir occasionally until melted. The coating is then ready to be molded. Cooling is unnecessary. If you wish to mold real milk chocolate, you *must* temper it before molding. To add flavor to molded candy, melt chocolate and stir in a few drops of *concentrated* flavoring oil. To color chocolate, use powdered food coloring as it will not affect consistency of chocolate.

Although many types of molds will work in molding chocolate, clear plastic molds are best and will be the only ones discussed. There are two main categories of clear plastic molds: the flat-back mold and the three-dimensional mold. The flat-back mold will make candy shaped on one side and flat on the other. Some of these molds have grooves at the base to accommodate a sucker stick. Three-dimensional molds are two-piece molds that clip together with paper clips or other fasteners which allow you to make stand-up or fully shaped candy figures. Usually there are indentations in the molds to insure proper alignment. These molds come in two distinct styles: molds with an open base and molds which are closed when clipped together.

The clear plastic molds need to be clean and dry before filling with chocolate. Greasing, spraying or dusting is not necessary and would ruin the appearance of the finished candy. If molds are used for something else other than chocolate, however, such as marshmallow, jellies or cooked candies, they must be greased or sprayed with an oiling spray. If a mold is to be filled several times, it does not need to be cleaned between uses, as the chocolate will come out cleanly and leave the mold ready for filling. When finished with the mold, wash it in hot water. Detergent will eventually dry out the mold and may crack it.

Flat-Backed Molds

If you want a solid piece of candy, spoon (or use a candy funnel) the melted chocolate into the mold. Underfill rather than overfill mold as overfilling will cause a "foot" to form at the base of candy. Tap mold on the table to release air bubbles, or lift mold and work bubbles out with a toothpick. Fill all cavities in mold, then chill in freezer for a few minutes. Leave in freezer only long enough for chocolate to harden slightly. Remove from freezer, turn upside down and candy should fall out. If candy does not fall out, flex mold slightly or return to freezer.

For molds with a soft center, use a paintbrush or small spoon to line mold cavity with chocolate, using just enough for a strong layer. Chill mold in freezer long enough for chocolate to harden slightly. Remove from freezer and spoon soft center into the cavity, leaving a small rim of chocolate around top. Spoon a small amount of chocolate over top to seal, chill for a few minutes and unmold.

Three-Dimensional Molds

With three-dimensional molds, you can either make solid or hollow figures, as well as filled candy. For multicolored figures, follow directions given for chocolate painting, coloring each half of the mold before completing figure.

Molds that clip together and have a hole in the base are very easy to use. For a solid piece of candy, use plenty of paper clips to fasten the two halves together and spoon chocolate into mold until it is full. Prop mold up in freezer so chocolate will not run out the bottom. Chill only until the chocolate hardens slightly. Remove from freezer; take paper clips off and carefully pull mold apart. If chocolate oozed into the seam, trim with a sharp knife.

To make hollow figures, fill mold only about one-half full, then turn mold from side to side until chocolate coats entire mold. Chill in freezer for a short time. Before chocolate hardens, remove and again turn from side to side to insure a thick layer of chocolate on the bottom. Repeat if necessary. Finally, remove from freezer and unmold as before. If you wish to have a soft candy center inside a hollow piece, fill figure before unmolding. Then cover bottom with chocolate so center will not be exposed to air.

Assorted painted molded candies for holidays.

Candy Molding Basics

There are many ways to use three-dimensional molds that come in sheets. If a solid figure is desired, prepare one half as for a solid, flat piece of candy. When this piece is made, fill other half with warm chocolate. Carefully position this piece over warm chocolate, making sure there is enough to make a good seal and the piece is aligned correctly. Chill in freezer for a few minutes, then unmold.

To make hollow figures, follow directions above, but instead of filling each half of the mold, use a paintbrush or spoon to make a thick layer of chocolate on mold. If you wish a soft center using this mold, paint each half of mold, and chill in freezer with halves apart. Then spoon the center inside the cavity. Paint fresh chocolate around edge of one mold. Leave this piece in the mold; remove other piece and position over first piece. Chill and unmold.

A hollow figure can also be made with these molds by filling one side of mold with soft chocolate, clipping the two halves together securely, and then rotating mold until completely covered. Chill for a short time, but remove before chocolate hardens. Rotate again for an even coat. Chill to harden and unmold.

Chocolate-Covered Cherries

These can be made using Dry Fondant, No-Cook Fondant or Cream Cheese Fondant. The acid in cherries causes the fondant to liquefy. They can be covered with chocolate in one of two ways: by dipping in melted chocolate or using bonbon molds. Be sure to thoroughly cover the cherries with chocolate.

Makes 48.

> Real milk chocolate, melted for dipping
> 48 maraschino cherries, drained, patted dry
> Dry Fondant *or* No-Cook Fondant *or* Cream Cheese Fondant

Melt chocolate in double boiler over hot, not boiling, water. Pour to top of 48 bonbon molds. Place rack over molds; invert quickly over baking sheet so excess chocolate drips out of mold allowing thin coating to remain. (Chocolate drippings can be returned to top of double boiler.) After 3 to 4 minutes, invert mold; draw small metal spatula across top of each cavity to level. Freeze 4 to 5 minutes; fill with fondant-covered cherry. Fill each with melted chocolate to top of cavity; freeze until set. Pop out of molds; place in paper cups; store in tightly covered tin.

Note: If you do not have bonbon molds, dip each fondant-covered cherry in melted chocolate; place on waxed paper to set. Check in 2 hours for leaks or areas that are not completely covered with chocolate. Seal by brushing with melted chocolate, if necessary. Place in paper cups; store in tightly covered tin.

Dry Fondant

> Dry fondant
> Maraschino cherry juice

Spread dry fondant on baking sheet. Fill atomizer-type bottle with maraschino cherry juice. Roll each of 48 small maraschino cherries in dry fondant until well covered. Place on a separate baking sheet; spray with cherry juice to moisten. Roll in dry fondant once again; return to baking sheet. Continue spraying and rolling in fondant until cherries are thoroughly coated.

No-Cook Fondant

> 3 tablespoons butter *or* margarine
> ¾ cup marshmallow creme
> 1 tablespoon invert sugar
> ½ teaspoon almond extract
> ¼ teaspoon vanilla
> Dash salt
> 2½ cups sifted confectioners' sugar
> 3 drops invertase, optional

Beat butter and marshmallow creme in large bowl. Add next 4 ingredients, 1¼ cups confectioners' sugar and invertase, if desired. Beat well; gradually add remaining 1¼ cups confectioners' sugar. (If dough is sticky, add more confectioners' sugar to make stiff dough.) Wrap in plastic wrap; refrigerate until ready to use. Bring to room temperature before using. To use, pinch off small pieces of No-Cook Fondant; wrap around each of 48 small maraschino cherries using your fingers.

Note: Invertase will make fondant in Chocolate-Covered Cherry liquefy in about 5 days.

Cream Cheese Fondant

> 1 3-ounce package cream cheese, room temperature
> 3 tablespoons butter, room temperature
> Dash salt
> ¼ teaspoon almond extract
> ¼ teaspoon vanilla
> 2½ to 3 cups confectioners' sugar

Mix cream cheese and butter in mixing bowl using wooden spoon. Add next 3 ingredients; blend well. Stir in confectioners' sugar gradually. Turn out onto counter; knead until dough is no longer sticky and can be formed into smooth ball. Divide into 3 parts; form each into 1¼-inch diameter log. Wrap in plastic wrap; refrigerate until ready to use. Bring to room temperature before using. To use, slice logs into ⅛-inch slices. Flatten each of 48 slices; place small maraschino cherry in center of each. Form fondant around cherry using your fingers. Roll in palms of hands to form round balls.

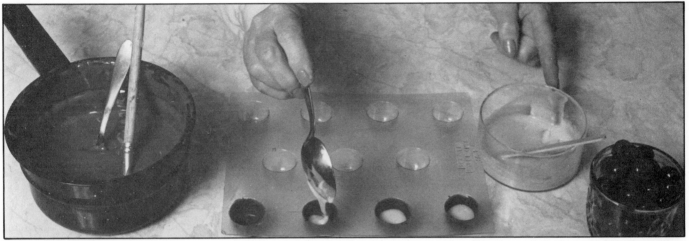

Pour liquid fondant into chocolate painted mold.

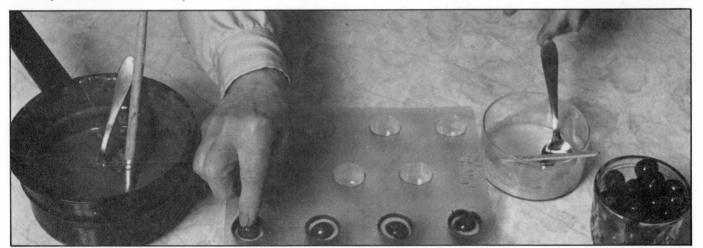

Place cherry into liquid fondant.

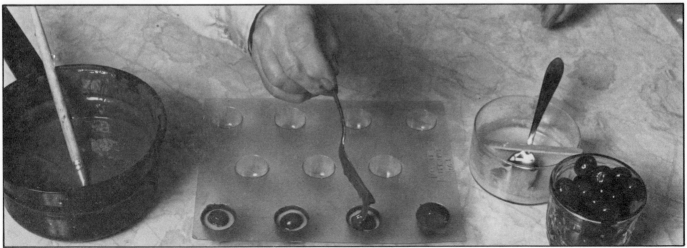

Cover cherry and fondant with chocolate.

Candy Bars

Candy Bars

There is no end to the variety of candy bars one can create. A few recipes are provided. By combining homemade or purchased caramel, marshmallow, nougats or fondants, nuts, raisins, cereal, etc. you can make your own original candy bar creations.

Line candy bar molds with a brush or by filling full of chocolate, inverting on a rack, then trimming the excess from around each mold as described in "Chocolate-Covered Cherries." While chocolate is still soft, pat in soft filling or cut firmer filling to size and fit into the chocolate shell. Or let the chocolate shell set first, then fill. Add caramel or marshmallow for the top layer, if desired. Seal carefully with more soft chocolate, chill, then unmold. Wrap individually. Slice to serve.

To avoid the brittle texture of chocolate, add 1½ tablespoons paramount crystals or 1½ tablespoons corn oil to each pound of melting chocolate and blend it in well. Proceed as described above.

Silky Way Bars

Makes approximately 20.

1 pound milk chocolate-flavored compound coating, wafers *or* pieces
3 tablespoons water
1¼ cups marshmallow creme
¼ pound caramel
½ pound (approximately) real milk chocolate, melted for coating

Melt chocolate-flavored compound coating in double boiler over hot water. Add water and marshmallow creme; blend well. Cool until mixture can be easily handled. Melt caramel in double boiler over hot water and cool. Line candy bar molds with melted chocolate; chill until firm but not set so chocolate does not crack. When firm spoon a thin layer of cooled caramel in bottom of shell. Pat chocolate-marshmallow filling on top of caramel to within ¹⁄₁₆-inch of top. Seal with additional melted chocolate. Chill; pop out when set.

Deluxe Chocomel Candy Bars

Makes 12 1½-inch round candy bars *or* 21 1 x 2⅓-inch candy bars *or* 60 bonbons.

1¾ cups very finely chopped real milk chocolate
2 tablespoons prepared Water Fondant (Recipe on page 20)
2 tablespoons frozen nondairy coffee creamer, thawed and warmed slightly
1½ tablespoons honey
Few grains salt
¼ teaspoon vanilla
Butter *or* vegetable oil spray
½ pound caramel, purchased *or* homemade
1 cup salted blanched peanuts
1 pound (approximately) real milk chocolate, melted for dipping
Peanuts, for garnish, if desired

Melt 1¾ cups milk chocolate and fondant separately in double boiler over hot water; then combine. Quickly add creamer, honey, salt and vanilla; blend well. Lightly butter or spray 12 1½-inch round molds *or* 7-inch square pan which has been lined with foil *or* 60 smooth bonbon molds. Quickly spoon candy into molds or pan; spread smooth. Cut a thin slice of caramel; stretch to desired thinness to fit candy bars. Place 4 to 5 peanuts on candy in molds; cover with caramel. Chill until set. Immediately remove from molds and place on foil to dry. When dry, dip in melted chocolate. Decorate with additional peanuts while chocolate is soft, if desired.

Clockwise, from Top: Hand-Dipped Snackers Bars and Molded Snackers, page 52; Deluxe Chocomel Candy Bars (patties), this page; Undipped Snackers (center); Almond Polar Bars, page 52; Chewy Coconut Bars, page 53; Almond Polar Bar; Creme de Menthe Candy Bars, page 52.

Candy Bars

Snackers Bars

Makes 60.

First Layer

    3 tablespoons dry egg whites
    2 tablespoons water
    ¼ cup invert sugar
    2 cups granulated sugar
    ⅓ cup water
    ⅔ cup invert sugar
    1 cup light corn syrup
      Dash salt
    ½ cup smooth peanut butter
    2 tablespoons vegetable shortening
    1 teaspoon vanilla

Combine egg whites with 2 tablespoons water; beat with electric mixer until light and fluffy. Gradually add ¼ cup invert sugar; continue to beat until mixture forms soft peaks. Set aside. Combine granulated sugar, ⅓ cup water, ⅔ cup invert sugar, corn syrup and salt in heavy saucepan; cook to 250° on a candy thermometer. Pour 1⅛ cups syrup mixture over beaten egg whites; blend well. Cook remaining syrup mixture to 285°; add to egg white mixture and continue beating with mixer. Add peanut butter; beat until mixture forms soft peaks. Blend in shortening and vanilla. Pour into buttered 9 x 13-inch pan. When cool, pour second layer on top.

Second Layer

    1 cup butter
    1 pound light brown sugar
    ⅛ teaspoon salt
    1 cup light corn syrup
    1 can sweetened condensed milk
    1 teaspoon vanilla
    2 cups chopped, blanched salted peanuts
    1 pound (approximately) real milk chocolate, melted for dipping

Melt butter in heavy 3-quart saucepan. Stir in sugar and salt; bring to boil. Add corn syrup; bring to boil. Add milk; cook to 245° on a candy thermometer, stirring constantly and lowering heat as mixture thickens. Remove from heat; stir in vanilla and nuts. Pour over first layer. When cold, cut into bars and dip in melted chocolate or fit into chocolate-lined candy bar molds.

Note: 1½ to 2 pounds ready-made caramels can be melted and substituted for second layer.

Choco-Mallow Candy Bar Filling

Makes 10 to 12 bars.

    1 cup finely chopped real milk chocolate
    ¾ cup marshmallow creme

Melt chocolate in double boiler over hot water. Add marshmallow creme; blend well. Refrigerate until firm enough to handle; pat into chocolate-lined candy bar molds and seal with melted chocolate or a combination of melted chocolate and crushed graham crackers.

Almond Polar Bars

Makes approximately 20.

    1 pound white compound coating, wafers *or* pieces
    3 tablespoons water
    ¾ cup marshmallow creme
    2 cups whole roasted almonds
    ½ pound (approximately) white compound coating, melted for dipping

Melt 1 pound compound coating in double boiler over hot water. Add water, marshmallow creme and almonds; blend well. Chill until firm enough to handle easily. Line candy bar molds with ½ pound melted compound coating; chill to set. Fill nearly to top with almond filling; seal with additional melted compound coating. Chill; pop out when set.

Creme de Menthe Candy Bars

Makes approximately 20.

    ½ pound real semisweet chocolate
    ½ pound real milk chocolate
    ½ cup whipping cream
    ¼ cup corn oil
    ¼ teaspoon peppermint oil
    ¾ tablespoon creme de menthe flavoring
    1 pound (approximately) green compound coating, wafers *or* pieces, melted

Melt semisweet and milk chocolates together in double boiler over hot water. Combine cream, corn oil and flavorings in separate saucepan; heat to 120° on a candy thermometer. Add all at once to melted chocolates; beat until smooth. Set aside. Line candy bar molds with melted compound coating; chill to set. Fill with chocolate mixture. Seal bottom with additional compound coating; chill to set. Unmold candy bars.

Crunchy Layered Candy Bars No. 1

Makes 20.

1½ cups granulated sugar
½ cup light corn syrup
¼ cup water
1 cup smooth peanut butter
½ pound (approximately) real milk chocolate, melted for dipping

Combine sugar, corn syrup and water in heavy saucepan; cook to 285° on a candy thermometer. Remove from heat; quickly stir in peanut butter. Pour onto buttered surface. Score into bar shapes while hot. When cool, dip in melted chocolate.

Crunchy Layered Candy Bars No. 2

Makes 15.

¾ cup light corn syrup
½ cup smooth peanut butter
½ pound (approximately) real milk chocolate, melted for dipping

Place corn syrup in small saucepan; cook to 288° on a candy thermometer. Remove from heat; quickly add peanut butter. Pour onto buttered marble slab or cookie sheet. When cool, carefully cut into bar shapes. Dip in melted chocolate or fit into chocolate-lined candy bar molds.

Candy Bar Filling

Makes approximately 70 bars.

1 cup granulated sugar
1 cup light brown sugar
1 cup light corn syrup
1 cup water
¼ cup dry egg whites
3 tablespoons water
¼ cup real semisweet chocolate, melted*
1 teaspoon vanilla

Combine sugars, corn syrup and 1 cup water in heavy saucepan. Cover; bring to boil, watching closely so mixture does not boil over. Remove lid; cook to 238° on a candy thermometer. Meanwhile, combine egg whites and 3 tablespoons water in bowl. Before syrup mixture reaches 238°, start to beat egg white mixture. Add cooked syrup slowly to egg whites; continue to beat until thick and fluffy. Fold in melted chocolate and vanilla. Immediately fill chocolate-lined candy bar molds or cool, wrap in plastic wrap and store for later use. (Moistening or buttering hands makes it easier to work with soft candy mixture.)

Variation

Caramel and Nut Filling: Use Candy Bar Filling in layers along with caramel and nuts in chocolate-lined candy bar molds.

Note: For a white center, substitute white compound coating for real semisweet chocolate.

Chewy Coconut Bars

Makes approximately 10 small bars *or* 20 pieces.

½ cup light corn syrup
¼ cup invert sugar
⅛ teaspoon salt
2 cups desiccated coconut
½ teaspoon vanilla
Chocolate shells *or* ½ pound (approximately) pastel compound coating, wafers *or* pieces, melted for dipping

Combine corn syrup, invert sugar and salt in heavy saucepan; heat to 208° on a candy thermometer. Remove from heat; add coconut and vanilla. Blend well. Let cool; press into chocolate shells which have been made from molds or roll into balls and dip in melted compound coating.

Cornstarch Molds

Cornstarch Molds

To prepare the cornstarch for molding, sift 4 pounds of cornstarch into a 9 x 13-inch pan; *do not pack.* Place in warm oven (250°F) 30 minutes until it is perfectly dry. Fluff the cornstarch with a wire whisk. Level with a yardstick. Choose molds with simple designs. Press molds carefully into cornstarch in pan. (Pan will hold 20 to 30 centers.) Lift mold straight up so imprint of mold remains in cornstarch. Fill cavities with warm liquid centers; sift cornstarch generously over top of centers. The cornstarch forms a crust on the soft centers. Leave centers in cornstarch several hours or overnight (not too long or they will dry out completely). Lift centers from cornstarch, lightly rubbing off cornstarch with hands. Handle very carefully as centers are delicate. Remove any excess cornstarch with a soft brush. Dip in melted chocolate. Recipe yields are approximate, depending on size of cavity.

Commercial Gumdrops

Makes 30.

　½ cup powdered gum arabic
　½ cup hot water
1¼ cups granulated sugar
　Few grains salt
　¼ teaspoon cream of tartar
　½ cup hot water
　3 drops oil of cinnamon *or* other flavoring oil
　Red food coloring *or* other food color
　¾ pound white compound coating, melted for dipping

Dissolve gum arabic in ½ cup hot water in top of double boiler. Strain mixture into bowl. Wash top of double boiler and return strained mixture to it. Cook sugar, salt, cream of tartar and hot water in small covered saucepan. When mixture is boiling rapidly, remove lid, insert candy thermometer and cook without stirring to 270°. Pour into gum arabic mixture; stir to blend and leave in double boiler over boiling water for 35 minutes. Skim foam from top. Add flavoring and coloring. Pour into small measuring cup; then pour into prepared cornstarch molds. Sift cornstarch generously over top of candies to cover well. Let stand at least 3 days. Lift gumdrops from cornstarch and carefully dust off excess cornstarch. Dip in melted compound coating. Keep gumdrops right side up and slide off end of fork.

Cherry Centers

Makes 20 to 30.

　½ recipe Water Fondant (Recipe on page 20)
　2 tablespoons maraschino cherry juice
　¼ teaspoon almond flavoring
　Real milk chocolate, melted for dipping

Heat all ingredients except chocolate in double boiler over hot water to 110° on a candy thermometer. Pour into small measuring cup or parchment bag and fill prepared cavities in cornstarch. Sift cornstarch on top. Let set several hours or overnight. Remove centers from cornstarch and dust excess cornstarch off. Dip in melted chocolate.

Variation

Mocha Centers: Prepare as above using 1 tablespoon instant coffee and 1 tablespoon boiling water in place of maraschino cherry juice and almond flavoring.

Grape Centers

Makes 20 to 30.

　2 cups dry fondant
　3 tablespoons unsweetened grape juice
　Real milk chocolate, melted for dipping

Dissolve dry fondant in grape juice in double boiler over hot water; heat to 110° on a candy thermometer. Pour into small measuring cup or parchment bag and fill prepared cavities in cornstarch. Sift cornstarch on top. Let set several hours or overnight. Remove centers from cornstarch and dust excess cornstarch off. Dip in melted chocolate.

Variation

Orange Centers: Prepare as above using 2 tablespoons frozen orange juice concentrate and 1½ tablespoons water in place of grape juice.

Top Tier: Molded Chocolate-Covered Cherries, page 48; Bottom Tier: Hand-Dipped Chocolate Cherries, page 48. Small Dish: Commercial Gumdrops, this page.

Painting Molds

Chocolate Painting

Very attractive multicolored chocolate candies can be molded using clear plastic molds. Melt the colors you wish to use in at least one-pound quantities in separate double boilers, or put small amounts of different colors of chocolate in small glass jars and place jars in a hot water bath. Different colors of chocolate can also be placed in the separate cavities of a cupcake pan which is then placed in a hot water bath. In either case, be careful not to get water in chocolate.

When chocolate melts, color it with paste or powdered food coloring *(do not use liquid food coloring)* to produce a darker color or a color not available in chocolate compound coatings. Too much color will make the chocolate thick and difficult to use and may prevent it from setting up shiny. If chocolate becomes thick, add a few paramount crystals or liquid vegetable oil. Use compound coating or chocolate that is nearest the color you desire. If you want red, start with pink compound coating; if you want black, start with dark chocolate.

Once chocolate is melted, apply it with paintbrushes which will not lose their bristles. Paint directly onto mold, using one color at a time, then chilling it for a few minutes to harden. Paint every other area, letting chocolate set slightly, then go back and paint areas between to keep colors from running together. Continue painting and cooling until all the parts of the mold you wish colored are painted. Then fill mold completely with slightly cooled chocolate. Chill mold in freezer until it hardens slightly; turn out candy.

Painting a mold.

Molded Candy Boxes

Molded Candy Boxes

Beautiful molds are available for making gift boxes of chocolate. A box of candy with the box edible as well as its contents is a very unique gift. Heart-shaped or other shaped 6-, 7- or 8-inch pans also can be used as chocolate molds and make attractive edible gift boxes. Use the plastic molds available as you would any mold. Line the box and lid with chocolate, brushing it on thickly. Let set in a cold place. Apply a second coat to reinforce it and let it set. To level the top edge of the box and the edge of the lid, place a cookie sheet on a burner, using lowest heat on an electric stove or pilot light only on a gas stove. Handle chocolate box carefully to minimize fingerprints and turn upside down, melting the top edge to an even smoothness. Smooth edge of the lid the same way.

To use a heart or other shaped pan as a form for a box, grease bottom and sides and line the bottom with a piece of waxed paper or parchment paper a little bigger than the pan's bottom, slitting around the edge so it fits smoothly in the bottom and an inch or so up the sides. Attach with a little shortening. Now cut a strip of waxed paper or parchment paper to fit the sides of the pan and attach with shortening. Line the paper-lined pan with melted chocolate, using a wide brush. Chill and coat a second time to reinforce. When completely set, remove from pan and peel paper from chocolate. Level top of box as described above.

To make a lid for this box, spread chocolate over paper to about 1/16-inch thickness. Trace a pattern in the chocolate like the shape of the pan, 1/4-inch larger than the pan. When chocolate is partially set, cut out lid. Decorate with other small molded candies or chocolate piped with a parchment bag and tube or chocolate molded into roses or other flowers.

Piped Chocolate-Peanut Butter Roses

Use to decorate chocolate boxes or cakes.

1 cup melted real semisweet chocolate *or* any other real chocolate
1/3 cup smooth peanut butter
2 tablespoons hot water

Combine all ingredients; beat until smooth. Pipe roses, using a pastry bag and decorating tube, on a flower nail; remove with thin spatula or shears either to where they are to be used or onto waxed paper for later use.

Note: Mixture can be piped into borders or rosettes. Place a dry-roasted peanut into the center of each rosette, if desired.

Chocolate Molding Compound

Use to make hand-molded flowers.

2 tablespoons glucose *or* light corn syrup
1/2 cup melted real milk chocolate

Warm the glucose and add to the melted chocolate; mix until well blended. Cool slightly; wrap in waxed paper or plastic wrap and let stand in cool place until firm. *Do not refrigerate.* Break off small pieces; working quickly with fingers until pliable, shape into petals for a rose or other flower. Rubbing the petal briefly before attaching to the flower brings out a shine. Work very quickly with each petal or the warmth of your hands will melt the chocolate and the petal will "wilt." You need no "glue" to attach petals to the flower as the petal will be slightly softened and will adhere to the flower when a slight pressure is applied.

Note: Any flavor real chocolate *or* compound coating (light, dark *or* pastel) may be used.

Chocolate for Piping Borders

2 tablespoons hot water
1 cup melted semisweet chocolate

Add hot water to chocolate; beat smooth. Keep mixture warm over hot water. Pipe borders onto chocolate boxes.

Note: Mixture can be piped into rosettes. Place a whole roasted filbert into the center of each rosette, if desired.

Decorative Borders and Flowers for Chocolate Boxes and Eggs

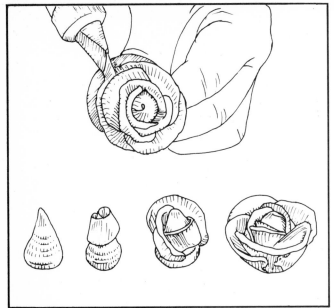

Various stages of an open rose.

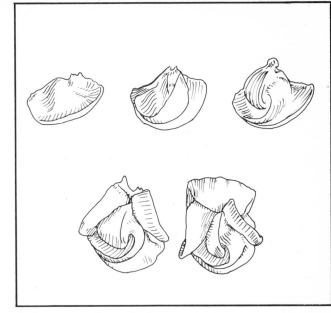

Various stages of a rosebud.

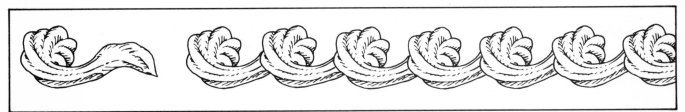

Scroll Border.

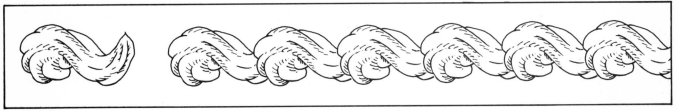

C-Scroll Border.

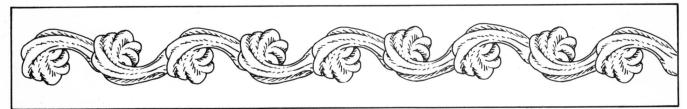

Reverse Scroll Border.

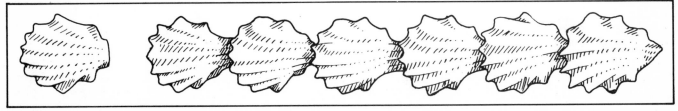

Shell Border.

Garnishes

Garnish with Chocolate

Alleghetti Frosting (sometimes called Shadow Icing) is an easy way to dress up plain frosting. In a small saucepan combine 1 square (1 ounce) unsweetened chocolate and ½ teaspoon shortening. Heat over low heat, stirring constantly. Drizzle melted chocolate from a teaspoon around the edge of the cake to form "icicles."

Curls—Draw blade of vegetable parer over smooth side of a slightly warm block of unsweetened baking chocolate or a dark, sweet chocolate bar.

Cutouts—Melt 4 ounces semisweet and 1 ounce unsweetened chocolate in the top of a double boiler over boiling water. Remove from heat, let cool 5 minutes, and stir with a wooden spoon until pan is cool to your touch.

Line cookie sheet with waxed paper and spread chocolate ³⁄₁₆ inch thick. Let cool until almost set. Press designs into chocolate, using cookie cutters. Peel paper from back of shape. Store on waxed paper in refrigerator.

Leaves—Gather 20 to 25 medium-size leaves with stems (English ivy, elm, dogwood). Wash and dry thoroughly. Melt 1 cup semisweet chocolate chips in top of double boiler over hot, not boiling, water. Remove from heat; keep over warm water. Carefully brush a thin layer (about ⅛ inch thick) of chocolate on underside of leaf. Chocolate and leaf will separate more easily if edges are not covered. Place coated leaves on wire rack until firm; chill if necessary. Carefully peel leaf from coating; store in cool place or refrigerator.

Using Molds for Other Foods

Butter Molds—Leave butter at room temperature for a few hours. Pack butter firmly into molds, a layer at a time, to eliminate air bubbles as much as possible. Pack mold completely full; freeze several hours or overnight. Flex mold and ease butter out. Work quickly so butter releases from mold before it softens. Cover and return butter to refrigerator until serving time. *Note:* Use butter, not margarine.

Dessert Cups—Many molds make attractive dessert cups. Simply line individual molds with thin layer of chocolate. Chill and remove from mold. Fill with ice cream, fluffy gelatin desserts, chocolate mousse, etc. The shallow shell mold is lovely as a base for ice cream with a second shell inverted at an angle over ice cream. One section of a three-dimensional Christmas tree mold is a lovely shape for a dessert shell. There are also square forms that adapt well for dessert shells.

Ice Cream Bars and Suckers—Ice cream bars and suckers can be made easily. Line molds with chocolate and let set. Quickly pack chocolate shells with firm ice cream being careful to leave a rim around top for sealing. Place in freezer to harden. Remove from freezer and quickly seal with chocolate that has been melted and allowed to cool. Store in freezer until serving time.

Gelatin Dessert Molds—Fruit-flavored gelatin made plain or with fruit, nuts, etc. is lovely using clear plastic molds. Any suitable clear plastic mold will work. Spray mold lightly with vegetable oil spray and wipe off excess with paper towel. Make gelatin according to directions on box except use ½ cup less water for each 3-ounce package. Pour dissolved gelatin into mold and let set several hours. Run point of sharp knife around mold. Immerse mold in warm running water for a few seconds. Place serving plate over mold and invert. If mold is still not releasing, work one edge loose with knife.

Rice Molds—Cook rice until dry and fluffy. On electric range, use 1 cup rice, 2 cups cold water and 1 teaspoon salt. Bring to a boil in covered pan. When boiling rapidly and steam is coming from under lid, turn burner off and leave on burner, covered, 30 minutes. If using a gas range, the rice will need to be simmered 30 minutes. The kernels will be fluffy and separated. Spray mold with vegetable oil spray. Pack rice tightly into mold; chill and turn out.

Mashed Potato Bars—Use leftover mashed potatoes or cook potatoes, mash and cool. It is important that potatoes are beaten quite dry. Instant mashed potatoes can be used, but potatoes cooked from scratch work best. Form logs approximately same size as mold you are using. Roll mashed potato log in finely crushed soda crackers, press into bar mold (or other mold) and turn out immediately. Place on buttered cookie sheet. Drizzle melted butter generously over potato bars. Bake in 400° oven 5 minutes. Place under broiler for additional 3 or 4 minutes or until nicely browned. Serve immediately. These can be made ahead of serving time, then finished at the last minute.

Ingredients

Acetic Acid—A strong vinegar concentrate available at a pharmacy.

Almond Paste—A smooth, heavy dough made of ground almonds. Used in candies and pastries.

Brown Sugar—Light brown sugar is milder in flavor and better than dark for most candy recipes. Pack brown sugar firmly when measuring.

Caramel—Can be purchased in block form. Made by the Nestle company and the Merkins company.

Chocolate Compound Coatings—Available from many companies in sweet, semisweet, butterscotch, peanut butter and a variety of colors for great versatility in candy making. Eliminates the tempering process necessary for real chocolate.

Citric Acid—Helps prevent sugaring and improves flavors, especially in fruit candies. Comes in liquid or crystal powder form. Crystals can be mixed with an equal amount of water to form liquid citric acid.

Coconut Dough—A chewy, coconut filling for candy bars or centers.

Coconut Oil—One of the ingredients in man-made chocolate. Used to thin chocolate or soften finished candy and make it less brittle.

Corn Syrup—Light corn syrup should be used in candy.

Cream—For these recipes, use heavy cream (whipping cream) unless otherwise noted.

Desiccated (Macaroon) Coconut—A finely cut, dry, unsweetened coconut.

Dry Corn Syrup—Corn syrup which has been dried to a powder. Do not reconstitute. To substitute for liquid corn syrup, add 5 parts dry corn syrup to 1 part water by weight. Heat over low heat until dissolved.

Dry Egg Whites—Reconstitute by adding 8 ounces dry egg whites to 1 pint water. Mix at slow speed until well blended. Gradually add 2½ pints water and mix well. Use 2 tablespoons reconstituted egg white for each egg white in the recipe.

Dry Fondant—A commercial powdered cane sugar product that needs to be reconstituted with liquids to make a simple fondant.

Flavorings—Many available for a vast variety in candy making. Flavorings are added full strength. Flavoring oils and concentrated flavorings are added by the drop and are desirable as they do not change the consistency of the candy when added.

Food Coloring—Available in paste and powder. Vivid colors can be obtained by using this type of coloring. Powder is best for chocolate.

Glucose—Concentrated corn syrup.

Heath Crunches—Include peppermint, toffee, pecan crisp, lemon and cinnamon. Ready to add to chocolate to make barks and fillings.

Invert Sugar—Cane sugar in liquid form. Improves the quality and keeping properties in candy. If it crystallizes, place over hot water until it liquefies.

Invertase—A yeast derivative, used in fondant centers to make them creamier as the fondant ripens. Usually only a few drops are necessary. Can be omitted from any recipe.

Lecithin—An emulsifier made from soybeans and used to keep oils from separating.

Maraschino Cherries—Available in small to medium size in 2-quart jars.

Milk Chocolate—A combination of chocolate liquor, added cocoa butter, sugar and milk or cream. It must contain at least 10% chocolate liquor. It may also contain optional ingredients.

Nondairy Liquid Coffee Creamer—The frozen liquid type is excellent in candy. Use in place of milk or cream in fudges.

Oils and Flavorings—Oils have a more potent flavor and do not thin candy. To flavor hard candies or chocolate, always use oils or very concentrated flavorings.

Paramount Crystals—Vegetable oils, mostly coconut oil, in small solid pieces and used as coconut oil.

Paste Food Coloring—Very concentrated food coloring obtained from cake-decorating stores.

Raw Chip Coconut—Unsweetened coconut in wide strips, used to make excellent brittle.

Semisweet Chocolate—A combination of chocolate liquor, added cocoa butter and sugar. It must contain at least 35% chocolate liquor. Most commonly known in the form of semisweet chocolate chips.

Sugar—Granulated cane sugar.

Sweet (Dark) Chocolate—A combination of chocolate liquor, added cocoa butter and sugar. It must contain at least 15% chocolate liquor and has a higher proportion of sugar than semisweet chocolate.

Toasted Coconut—Fine, sweetened golden brown coconut.

Equipment

Boxes—Candy gift boxes are available for any occasion in many shapes, sizes and colors.

Brushes—Brushes are an important tool in mold work, and only those recommended for foods should be used. A good quality brush which will not shed bristles is also important.

Candy Cups—Many colors and sizes can be purchased, both paper and foil.

Candy Thermometers—A necessary piece of equipment. The flat type with 2 degree separations is best because of the metal strip on the bottom with which you can stir candy. For use in the microwave and also for use when tempering chocolate, there is a good disc-type thermometer available which is fast-adjusting.

Cellophane Bags—These bags come in several sizes and are ideal for wrapping suckers.

Dipping Forks—A variety of styles with which to dip chocolate is available.

Double Boiler—Many kinds are on the market. Usually a small one is most efficient. Can be of granite, glass or stainless steel.

Marble Slab—The best surface for cooling candy. The best size is about 18 x 28 x 1 inch because it's not too heavy to handle.

Molds—Thousands of molds are available in plastic, metal, wood, ceramic, etc. With a little search, a mold can be found for nearly any occasion. The clear plastic molds are the most widely used in candy making at this time.

Wrappers—Foil squares in a variety of colors can be purchased to add color and sparkle to a box of candy.

Suggestions for Easy and Delicious Candy or Cookies Using the Coatings

Dip graham crackers in chocolate.

Dip pretzels in pastel compound coatings or chocolate.

Dip vanilla wafers in butterscotch compound coating or chocolate.

Dip Ritz (or similar crackers) in butterscotch compound coating or chocolate which has been flavored with a few drops of peppermint oil.

Sandwich soda crackers together with peanut butter; dip in chocolate.

Insert small sucker stick in the filling of "double stuff" cookies; dip in chocolate and decorate with small candies to make eyes and mouth.

Crush graham crackers and add to melted chocolate. Fill paper candy cups, drop in clusters or mold in candy bar molds.

Put thin slices of purchased caramel or your own homemade caramel between graham crackers and coat with chocolate.

Fasten sugar wafers together with chocolate or buttercream frosting. Dip in white, pastel or chocolate-flavored compound coating for quick petits fours.

Stir natural cereal into a favorite coating to make quick and delicious crunchy candy.

Melt peanut butter compound coating and add crisp rice cereal. Spread out on waxed paper and break into pieces when set.

Try the new Heath crunches: Mix Toffee or Pecan Crunch in milk chocolate, Lemon Crunch in yellow compound coating, Cinnamon Crunch in pink compound coating.

Purchase block caramel and cut into small squares. Dip in milk chocolate.

Mix roasted, salted peanuts in milk chocolate-flavored compound coating and drop in clusters on waxed paper.

Mix raisins and/or peanuts in chocolate-flavored compound coating and drop in clusters on waxed paper.

Melt 1 pound pink compound coating; add 1 cup Heath cinnamon crunch and 1½ cups crisp rice cereal. Spread out on waxed paper. Drizzle with semisweet chocolate.

Assorted painted molded candies.

Index

CANDY BARS

Almond Polar Bars, 52
Candy Bar Filling, 53
Chewy Coconut Bars, 53
Choco-Mallow Candy Bar
  Filling, 52
Creme de Menthe
  Candy Bars, 52
Crunchy Layered Candy Bars
  No. 1, 53
Crunchy Layered Candy Bars
  No. 2, 53
Deluxe Chocomel Candy Bars, 50
Silky Way Bars, 50
Snackers Bars, 52

CARAMELS

Almond Caramels, 15
Caramels, 15
Chewy Candy, 16
Chocolate Caramels from
  Purchased Caramel, 17
Evaporated Milk Caramels, 16
Layered Butterscotch, 17
Layered Caramels, 16
Orange Caramels, 16
Peanut Butter Caramels, 15
Penny's Time-Saving
  Caramels, 16
Soft Caramels, 15

CRUNCHES

Almond Brittle, 33
Almond Popcorn Crunch, 32
Brown Sugar Toffee, 32
Butter Brickle, 32
Butterscotch, 33
Chocolate Almond Toffee, 31
Crunchy Nougat, 31
Deluxe Brittle, 31
Glazed Almonds, 32
Peanut Butter Crunch, 33
Rock Candy Suckers, 33
Sesame Seed Brittle, 32
Sugared Almonds, 31
Super Caramel Corn, 33

EASY CANDY

Butterscotch Nut Log, 9
Candy Cookies, 9
Candy Hash, 9
Cathedral Candies, 12
Cheesy Coconut Easter Eggs, 11
Cherry Coconut Creams, 12
Cherry Popcorn, 12
Choco-Peanut Butter Fudge, 13
Coconut Fudge, 13
Crispy Fudge Sandwiches, 9
Easy No-Cook Fondant, 11
Easy Pecan Rolls, 13
Fruit Nut Fudge, 13
Heath Crunch Candy, 8
Layered Mints, 11
Maple Nut Bars, 8

Marble Fudge, 13
Marshmallow Cups, 11
Peanut Butter Crispy Bars, 12
Peanut Butter-Marshmallow
  Eggs, 11
Peanut Butter Sandwiches, 8
Peanut Fudge Bars, 8
Pecan Caramel Chews, 8
Pink Cinnamon Crunch, 12
Raisin Clusters, 9

FONDANTS

Almond Vanilla Buttercreams, 22
Apricot Creams, 22
Basic Fondant, 20
Butterscotch Creams, 25
Caramel Creams, 21
Cherry Creams, 22
Chocolate Easter Eggs, 25
Chocolate Truffles, 24
Cocoa Mocha Creams, 22
Double Butter Creamy
  Centers, 21
Easter Egg Candies, 25
Easy Chocolate-Covered
  Creams, 24
French Chocolates, 22
Maple Creams, 24
Maple Syrup Creams, 24
Mocha Truffles, 24
Peanut Butter Fondant, 21
Rich Butter Fondant, 20
Strawberry Orientals, 21
Tri-Flavor Easter Eggs, 25
Water Fondant, 20
Water Fondant Fruit Centers, 20

FUDGE

Apple Fudge, 29
Black Walnut Fudge, 29
Buttermilk Candy, 29
Chocolate Fondant Fudge, 27
Coconut Maple Creams, 28
Creamy Butter Fudge, 28
Italian Delights, 28
Maple Nut Fudge, 27
Old-Fashioned White Fudge, 27
Peanut Butter Fudge, 28
Peanut Butter Squares, 29
Piña Colada Fudge, 28
Rich Cream Fudge, 27
Strawberry Jam Fudge, 29

MICROWAVE

Butterscotch Fudge, 45
Choco-Mallo Treats, 45
Creamy Fudge, 44
Crunchy Cups, 45
Five-Minute Fudge, 44
Microwave Peanut Butter
  Fudge, 44
Peanut Brittle, 44
Peanut Clusters, 44
Pecan Brittle, 45

MINTS

Bavarian Mints, 18
Buttermints, 18
Compound Chocolate Mints, 18
Cream Cheese Mints, 18
Cream Mints, 17
Mints, 18
Party Mints, 17

MISCELLANEOUS

Buttermilk Pralines, 43
Caramel-Mallow Roll-Ups, 40
Carmelo Swirl and
  Choco-Carmelo Swirl
  Candy, 34
Chocolate-Covered Cherries, 41
Chocolate Malted Milk
  Nougat, 37
Cream Cheese Fondant for
  Cherries, 43
Deluxe Commercial Nougat, 37
Easy Fondant for
  Dipping Fruit, 43
Fluffy Marshmallow Candy, 40
Gelatin Gumdrops, 36
Half-Baked Candy, 41
Homemade Sweetened
  Condensed Milk, 37
Invert Sugar, 38
Marshmallow Creme or
  Frappé, 36
Mint Marshmallows, 40
Nougat Loaf, 37
Pecan Chews, 34
Pecan Rolls, 38
Pistachio Nougat, 36
Popcorn Patties, 38
Puffed Wheat TV Snacks, 41
Quick Pralines, 41
Rocky Road Candy, 34
Sno-Caps, 40
Soft Maple Nougat, 36
Spiced Nuts, 43
Twisted Kentucky Creams, 34
Walnut Slices, 38

MOLDED CANDIES

Chocolate-Covered Cherries, 48
Chocolate Molding
  Compound, 57
Chocolate for Piping Borders, 57
Cornstarch Molds
  Cherry Centers, 54
  Commercial Gumdrops, 54
  Grape Centers, 54
  Mocha Centers, 54
  Orange Centers, 54
Piped Chocolate Peanut Butter
  Roses, 57